- INTRODUCTION -

Congratulations on your brand new puppy!

The day you bring your new puppy home is one of the happiest days that you will have in your life. Being a pet owner is a rewarding experience, not only for you but for your new ball of fur too. This small bundle of joy will have boundless amounts of energy, they will be very clumsy at first but will soon be trecking around with you, tailing along behind you everywhere you go.

Soon enough, you won't be able to imagine your life without him. His fluffy fur, wet nose and that tail wagging like nothing you've ever seen before.

Your newest partner in life will be your best friend for many years to come. They will be by your side through the thick and thin of all that life will throw at you. Your new puppy will listen to your feelings, offer a compassionate cuddle and show undying love for you.

And, you will do the same for him.

Being a pet owner does come with responsibilities, however. And by purchasing this book, you have already realized this, so well done. You are on your way to becoming a responsible pet owner.

However, just buying this book doesn't change anything at all. It is up to you to implement the suggestions in this guide. It is up to you to help your dog become the best dog they can be, and help them become a valued member of your community.

This won't happen overnight. There are no shortcuts and you will need to invest a lot of time into your training schedule. Sometimes it will feel like a drag, or perhaps a lost cause. Just know that it will all be worth it, and it does get easier.

You will need lots of patience, lots of love and most importantly, lots of trust. The new love of your life will need lots of your attention, especially in those important first few months, but the rewards will flow for years to come after implementing excellent habits for your pooch.

So whether you have a loveable Labrador, a prancing Poodle or a brave Bulldog... I am here to help. We are in this together and we will train your new puppy to be the best dog you've ever had.

Let's begin training!

Know Your Breed

Okay, now let's take a step back before we move forward. If you have already adopted your puppy, then you can skip ahead from this chapter. Or perhaps you could read on and get future advice on your next puppy selection (a future friend for your new puppy, anyone?)

This is probably the most important part of your decision to be a dog owner. The things I am about to go through will determine your happiness and your pet's happiness for many years to come.
You need to get this right the first time. I have seen it all too many times before. The classic story goes something like this:

1. Owner wants a dog.
2. Owner gets dream dog without any research or knowledge of that particular breed.
3. The dog comes home and begins playing up.
4. Owner wonders why, and gets frustrated.
5. Dog ruins shoes, yard and plants due to the owners lack of knowledge about exercise requirements, social requirements and lifestyle requirements.
6. The owner gives up the dog, blames the dog for all the problems.

This story is seen over and over again at the various Dogs Homes across the world. So many owners go into owning their first dog without doing any research about how much work is required to own that particular breed. In the end, their expectations of owning a dog aren't met so they end up giving the dog away.
This is not only heartbreaking for the new puppy, but also the owner.

Each breed of dog is so unique, some similar to each other, while others vary greatly to the others. So in this chapter, I will outline a few important factors that you need to think about before getting your next puppy.

Why are you getting a dog?

This is the first question I get people to ask themselves when they decide they would like to get a new puppy, or a second or third dog for that matter. People get dogs for all sorts of different reasons, but if you can outline why you would like a dog, it will go a long way into working out which type of dog you should get.

You might be looking to get a dog to keep you company on your long days at home alone, but you might not be able to take him on long walks.

Or, perhaps you have children and would like to get them a dog to help teach them responsibility and give them an upbringing like you had, with pets.

Your home might be very important to you, or you run a business from home and have extremely valuable things scattered around your yard. You decide to get a dog to scare away some unwanted visitors, you decide to get a guard dog.

Another scenario might be where you have been given strict guidelines about your weight, you need to lose weight for your health. You lack the motivation to get up and do something every day but if you had a dog, you would feel compelled to provide them with the love and exercise that they require, hence helping you with your weight loss goals.

Do you see why it is such an important question to ask yourself, at the very beginning of your puppy journey?

Let's say, for example, you wanted a dog for exercise to assist you in your weight loss goals. You go out to the pet store and see the cute little pug puppies, the breed of dog that you have always wanted. So you buy him, take him home and get to know him. Then, when he's a bit older you try to take him for a jog, to help you with your weight loss goals. You discover, that not only does he not like to run, but it is also dangerous for him to do the type of exercise that you are asking him to do.

To use another example, let's say you are a retired pensioner who has mobility issues. You require a walking frame to get from point-to-point. Your days are long and lonely, you don't like cats, so you decide to get a dog.

You see an ad while watching TV and you see a local breeder has some Border Collie puppies, and they are oh-so-cute! You head out to the breeder, and you purchase a brand new Border Collie puppy. You take him home and your bond is instant. That is until he gets bored and starts to chew all your expensive shoes and clothing. Then he digs holes in your yard and tramples through the garden beds, ruining all of your flowers.

After a short while, you decide you have had enough, he is a naughty dog and you take him to the shelter.

In both of these examples, if the owner had just asked themselves the simple question of why do I want a dog?, they could have made a more informed decision and saved the heartache of needing to take the dog to the Dogs Home to look for a new owner, simply because that type of dog didn't fit their lifestyle.

Below is a list that I have made, a quick rundown of this list should narrow down your selection substantially. All of the items are important things to consider.

They will all impact your life, and more importantly, your dog's happiness.

- How much time will I have to spend with my dog?
- How much time can I allow for exercising my dog?
- Where will I exercise my dog?
- What size is my home? Is there a yard or a place for them to go to the toilet?
- How busy is the household and how much will they interact with the dog?
- Are there small children to consider?
- Do I have any other pets?

Once you have gone through and answered these questions you will have started to gauge what type of dog you might be able to get, a dog that will fit into your lifestyle.

You can then ask yourself another series of questions to help narrow it down even further.

This list will help you start to get a real idea of the dog you could get, but contains important factors.

- What size dog would I like?
- Do I want a long or short haired dog?
- What about shedding? How many times a week can I brush my dog? (also consider allergies)
- How much will my dog bark? Will that cause issues? eg. with neighbors
- How independent do I want my dog to be?

Assessing all of these things will hopefully drop your list of potential breeds down to the bare minimum. Fingers crossed you have only two or three breeds to choose from after going through the above sequence of questions.

After you have made your final decision it is time to head to the Dogs Home, pet store or to a local breeder. Different people have different opinions on where you should get your dog, but that is a moral decision that only you can make. I hold no objectives to any of the above options, each person is different and you need to make a choice that you are comfortable with. Personally, I have bought a dog from a breeder and I have also adopted a dog from the Dogs Home.

One note I would make about going to a breeder is that you should check they are a verified breeder and not just someone running a breeding program in their backyard. Try to view the parents and where possible, if paying top dollar for a purebred puppy, get certificates to assure you are getting what you pay for.

Lifespans

One thing to touch on would be the life expectancy of your new best friend. Becoming a dog owner isn't something that you can just 'do' for a few weeks, or months or years. It is a long term commitment that you make.

However, there are different expectations that you should have once you have decided on your breed. As a general rule, small dogs live longer than the larger breeds. Take for example, the Chihuahua. The little cutie has a life expectancy of up to 18 years (sometimes longer, this is just an average!). That is a long time and a huge commitment on your behalf.

A German Shepherd has an average lifespan of 9-13 years, being a much more active and larger breed of dog. A Boxer also has a wide span of 8-15 years, quite similar to a Labrador Retriever.

As you can see, the life of a dog varies a lot between breeds. A lot of factors come into this, as it does with you and me as humans. Health, happiness, and lifestyle all contribute to a dog's life expectancy just as it does for you.

You can help your dog have a long, happy and fulfilling life by getting it right from the start.

Help by feeding your dog a healthy, balanced diet. This isn't something that I will go over in this book, but I would highly recommend doing some reading on this part of your dog's life too. It is just as important to your dog as it is to you. A healthy diet and exercise, no matter the breed, will go a long way to helping your dog live as long as possible. And be as happy as possible, too!

Intelligence

One final thing to note about choosing your dog is the intelligence variation between all the breeds. As with the lifespan, and much like us humans, a dogs intelligence varies greatly.

You have chosen to read this book to advance your education in training your dog. Unfortunately, your dog doesn't have the ability to read. It will be your sole responsibility to take care of his education.

If you have other pets around, namely older pets, they will also assist you in teaching your new puppy life's lessons. Although they will help, it won't be the same as you teaching your puppy firsthand.

As with all things you have learned so far, different breeds have different capabilities in terms of learning. You see Beagles often used for hunting because they have been used that way for centuries. It is bred into them and becomes instinct for them to do the things that they do.

Much the same as it is for Labradors to show love and compassion. There is a reason they are used worldwide as Guide Dogs. They have a love and affection that outweighs most other breeds and this is used to help everyday humans in their life.

You will only have a pet, though. Just know that there may be limitations on how much you can teach your puppy. Don't have the expectation of a St Bernard to be rolling along on a skateboard or a Toy Poodle to play fetch for hours.

- BEFORE YOUR PUPPY ARRIVES HOME -

PREPARE YOUR HOME AND YOUR MIND!

After you have chosen your puppy, it is possible that you might have to wait before you can bring him home. In some areas of the world, it is illegal to sell puppies before they reach 8 weeks of age.

In other areas, you may sell them before they reach this milestone, but they cannot leave their mothers until they reach 2 months of age anyway.

The main reason for this rule is because puppies need their mothers care and attention for those early weeks of their life. Your little puppy is fully dependant on their mother for food, and won't start eating proper puppy food until about 4 weeks of age.

It is around this age that the weaning process begins, separating the puppy from the mother gradually and teaching the puppy to fend for themselves. Your puppy will need to stay with his brothers and sisters so he can learn from them and begin to develop his social skills. There are some things that humans cannot teach young puppies, such as refraining from biting. This will be taught by his siblings or even his mother. When he begins to chomp down too hard his puppy family will be sure to let him know he is being too rough.

Puppies who are separated from their mothers too early may suffer major health issues later in life. It can also affect their coordination skills and their social skills too. It is critical to allow your puppy enough time to learn from his family, and I can't stress this enough.

By the time your puppy reaches 8 weeks old, you are normally permitted to bring him home. During this chapter, I will go through some things you can do beforehand to help make the transition for both you and your puppy go through seamlessly. These are things that you can do while you wait for your puppy to be ready to come home. Some require some work to be done to your home and others are simply setting some rules so everyone inside your home is on the same page as one another. Most of the things can be done over the course of a weekend, unless of course you need to do some serious puppy proofing of your backyard!

The Household Rules

It's an old school belief that all dogs must have a master. The belief that you should eat before your dog, enter the room before your dog and keep them off the furniture is dated, and only you decide what your puppies rules will be once he arrives into your home.

Although this is an old belief, I do believe that your dog must be aware that there are rules that they must obey. Just like if you have children, there are things you don't mind them doing, and things that you are absolutely against them doing. The same will go for your puppy.

I strongly encourage you to sit down before your puppy arrives and work out the rules. If you live with other people, or with other family members, get them to join you and listen to their ideas and their inputs. It is important that everyone feels comfortable inside the home, and that everyone understands what the dog is and isn't allowed to do. If you all sit down together, there will be no misunderstandings and everyone will know what you have agreed on. Puppies require consistency to learn quickly, so this is an important step in achieving consistent guidelines for your new family member.

It might help to write down the rules, this way everyone can refer back to them if they forget.

Below is a small list of things you might like to discuss with other people within your home. If you live alone, it will stay pay to have a think about what rules you would like your puppy to live by and it might still be a good idea to write down what you decide.

- Where in the house is the dog allowed? Are any rooms forbidden? Can they g upstairs and downstairs?
- Is your dog allowed to sit on the furniture?
- Does he get table scraps? Where will he sit while you are eating?
- Does he have to wait for you to say it's ok before going through a gate or entering the house?
- Who is responsible for feeding and checking water?

- Who cleans up the dedicated toilet area?
- Who is responsible for brushing and grooming?
- Who exercises your puppy? And how often?
- Is he allowed to jump on people?
- Where does he sleep? In a crate or wherever he pleases?

So you see, there are so many things that you will need to think about before he comes home. If you can answer at least some of these questions before he arrives it will save a lot of time and stress later. Not to mention any disagreements you might have with other members of your family.

Like any of the training you are about to undertake with your new puppy, consistency is key to his success. Everyone must agree to stick to the rules, no matter what. If your puppy gets a different answer from one person to the next, be it where he is going to the toilet or whether he is allowed under the table when you eat, he will start to get confused and this will cause issues with his learning. If your puppy gets away with something once, it is likely that they will continue to think they can get away with it forever.

The easiest way to avoid accidents is to make sure everyone is 100% behind the rules you decide on. It is the only fair way for everybody to live together under one roof happily.

Puppy Equipment and Supplies

Before the puppy comes home, I recommend stocking up on all the items that you will need for at least the first week. Not only does this include food, but also anything that you might require to assist with your training in those early days.

This will reduce any stress that is caused for you and your puppy by you having to leave the home to go and grab something from the store that you could have organized earlier. Don't go overboard though, you won't need a million toys for him to play with in the first week. You won't need endless amounts of kibble or whatever food you have decided to feed him.

Food & Feeding Bowls

I would recommend getting two weeks worth of kibble. This obviously depends on how much your puppy will be eating, but a simple way to avoid running out is to get the biggest bag of dry food to start with (try to get the same food that he had been eating while at the breeders home, this will help him ease into the transition). Make sure you are getting 'Puppy' food. Don't feed him adult dog food as he will be missing out on important nutrients that are loaded into the puppy foods.

You will be feeding your puppy regularly for a little while, and although it will only be small amounts it can add up very quickly. Depending on which breed you have adopted, he might be eating up to 4 times a day! So get a good quality feeding bowl, one for his food and a separate one for his water. If your yard is large, try to put a few water bowls around so that he can find one easily. If you are finding that your puppy is 'woofing' down his food, you can get a 'slow-eat' bowl which has obstacles in the way of his food so it takes him a little longer to work his way around the bowl.

It's important not to underfeed your puppy, and it is also just as important not to overfeed him (complicated I know!). If you are unsure how much to feed him, look at the back of the packaging that your kibble comes in, or better yet, ask a local vet or the breeder.

You can also get some raw meaty bones to be used as a treat, although it's not normally recommended to give your puppy a bone until he is about 12-16 weeks old. Make sure the bone you select is raw. Do not ever feed your dog cooked bones as these can splinter and cause choking hazards for your puppy. The best type of bones are meaty ones, although giving him a normal bone once a week is ok too. Giving your puppy too many raw bones can lead to constipation so be aware of this too.

Chewing bones will help alleviate the teething issues that arise when your puppy begins to get his adult teeth, this is normally between four and six months of age. His adult teeth will grow very quickly, so he will be doing all he can to relieve symptoms of teething.

Other foods that your puppy might like are: cooked meats (no bones), tinned tuna, tinned salmon, finely cut vegetables.

Most people are aware that you should never feed your dog chocolate because it is toxic to them... However! There are many other foods which you should never feed your puppy too, and as with humans, your dog might have allergies to something that is normally considered ok for dogs to eat. So, whenever giving him something new, watch him closely and make sure he is ok.

A brief list of toxic foods for dogs is: alcohol, onions, garlic, chocolate, caffeine, avocado, grapes, raisins, sultanas, currants, fruit seeds, corncobs, unripe tomatoes, mushrooms.

There are many other toxic foods so always be careful whenever feeding your puppy something new. If in doubt, ask someone or do a quick internet search. It is better to be safe than sorry and have to rush to the vet in an emergency.

Walking and Training Equipment

I strongly recommend getting all of your training equipment before you get your puppy home with you. Mainly so that you can start your training on the very first day he comes home. Remember, he learns very quickly so you should make the most of this while he is so young.

Again, there are so many different items out there than you can get for your new pooch. You might not know which sex you are getting, so perhaps getting a pink leash for isn't ideal if you are in this situation. More often than not, you will know which you are getting, so be it boy or girl, try to get the equipment matching accordingly.

Although you will not be walking him straight away, it's easier to get the leash now before he comes home anyway. You can still attach it to his collar and start getting him used to it. You should try and get some ID tags to attach to his collar, just in case your puppy proofing of the yard has been slightly lapsed and he makes an escape.

If you plan to use clicker training (see Clicker Training Chapter), get this now too so you can start straight away.

A breakdown list of items you may find useful for training and walking your puppy are:

- collar (with ID tags)
- leash
- harness
- clicker
- treat bag

Sleeping Equipment

Your puppy will need his own area that he feels safe going into for a rest or to sleep. Although the couch and your bed might be an option that you have decided is ok, it is always a good idea for him to have his own bed that he can access even when you are not home.

There are many types of dog beds that you can purchase these days, so take your time in choosing the correct type. Don't purchase a dog bed that is too small, leave enough room for him to grow into it. There are also warming beds and cooling beds, so keep in mind the climate in which your puppy will sleep... If he sleeps downstairs where it gets cold, perhaps buy a warming bed or add an extra blanket or two for him. On the other hand, if you know it gets hot where you plan to put his bed, maybe the cooling style beds would be better suited for your puppy.

If you plan on crate training your puppy, include this in his area. I highly recommend crate training but this is, of course, your choice. Getting a crate that he can grow into is a good idea. Although it will be way too big to start with, it is better to do this rather than buying a new crate as he grows. Firstly because they can get expensive, and secondly because your puppy will learn that his crate is his space. Once you take it away, he will need to get used to a new home and this could upset him.

Grooming Equipment

Though not essential in the first week, why not get these items while you're at the store getting everything else?

Again, like anything that you will do in the early days at home with your puppy, you can try to get him used to being brushed. There are many types and you might have to try a few different brushes before you find one that is effective at grooming your puppy properly.

Depending on the breed you may find you need a deshedding brush. This has finer bristles on the brush and can remove heavy amount of fur from your dog. This is great for breeds who have a thick double coat or for breeds that are heavy shedders.

Get a standard brush, a comb and a deshedding brush all at the same time. They will all come in handy and you can use them in combination with each other.

Also handy will be a bottle of puppy shampoo and conditioner. Be sure it is for puppies and not adult dogs. Puppies have more sensitive skin and this type of shampoo will lower the risk of causing any skin irritation.

Puppy Proofing Your Home

Puppies love to explore. Everything is new and interesting and the world is there for the taking. Puppy proofing your home is just as important as baby proofing your home - the same hazards apply.

Once your puppy comes home with you he becomes completely reliant on you to show him what is dangerous and what is safe. It is now your responsibility to prevent his exposure to harmful things, whether they are indoor or outdoors. Spread around your home are things that your puppy is looking to chew, eat or swallow. By proofing your home properly from the beginning, you can help prevent your puppy from getting stuck, injured or sick. Take away the worry and proof your home so that you and your puppy can focus on having fun and spending quality time together instead.

Don't be afraid to get down on all fours within your home, try and see exactly what your puppy is going to see. If you seem to be finding a lot of hazards, start making a list so you don't forget anything.

A list of things I always recommend checking are:

- Check coffee tables, shelves, and decorative items on the ground for things that are within reach. Can the items be knocked off easily, either by a bump or a wagging tail? Remove the items that you don't want to be chewed up and place them in a drawer instead. Items may include television remotes, vases, sculptures, plants or food.
- Check all wires that are exposed. These are all at high risk of being chewed on, and this will cause serious harm to your puppy. Try to elevate the wires out of reach, or hide them within cupboards or behind furniture that your puppy will be unable to move. You can purchase wire covers from the home improvement store, so if you are unable to hide them then use this as an alternative option.
- Hide away trash cans. You don't want your puppy to get into the bin while you turn your back. He might eat or swallow something dangerous and this is a sure way to an emergency visit to the vet. If you

can hide them away in a cupboard, get a secure lid that won't budge off if it is pushed over.

- Remove any mice traps or insect bait stations. These contain poison and will harm your puppy if he decides to chew on them.
- Window blind cords are a real temptation for puppies to pull and chew on. Tie these up so that they are out of reach. Not only could he pull on these and pull the entire blind down, but he could also get strangled in the cord if he decides to play with it.
- Keep doors closed to areas that you don't want him to go into. Areas such as toilets are a prime place for puppies to get up to no good... Think toilet paper all over the floor or drinking from the bowl. Close these doors when you aren't in the rooms to save any trouble in the areas.
- Head outside and check the yard the same way you have inside. Pick up any obscure items that might be dangerous to him, trim trees and check to make sure you don't have any toxic plants that he might take to.
- Walk along your fence line and check for gaps. If your puppy sees a hole in your fence, he will try to go through it. His curious nature means he will sniff these spots out so look carefully.
- Think about putting wire underneath your fence, just in case he is a digger. Puppies dig. There are no two ways about it, but if he digs and feels wire on his claws, it won't feel nice so he will stop. Run wire right the way around your fence line to stop any potential escapes from digging under the fence.

This may take a little while, but puppy proofing your home is one of the most important things you will do. It is your responsibility to keep him safe now, so don't skip on this step of the book. Take your time, ask for advice and always refer back to this chapter if you need a reminder on what to check.

- THE FIRST FEW WEEKS

\-

ONCE YOU BRING YOUR PUPPY HOME

It's finally time to bring your puppy home. After all the excitement of picking him out, whether at the breeders or at the Dogs Home, one of the most exciting days of your life is finally here.

Because we have already been through everything that you need to do before your puppy arrives home, you should be well equipped to make it easy for you both, and easy for whoever else might be living with you at home. We've puppy-proofed the house, you have all the right gear including food bowls, so you are good to go.

There are many things that will come up in the first few days, many of which you wouldn't have anticipated - but lucky for you, you have read this book and will know what to expect!

The Journey Home - Pup's First Car Ride

It is very common for most dog-owners-to-be to collect their puppies from their mothers. You will need a crate for your puppy to sit in on the way home. The ideal scenario is that you use the same crate that they will be sleeping in, as this introduces it to them very early on (insider tip: load it with treats before you leave so he begins to associate good things with the crate!). If you are unable to use the same crate it won't matter too much this time around, so don't stress too much on this point. Try to organize the crate before you leave home, the less you have to do when you get there the better.

Try to make the crate comfortable by laying some blankets down for him. Don't have any water bowls or toys in the crate, but if your journey is going to be long, then definitely take water and a bowl but make frequent stops so he can have a drink. Ignore any mess that he makes in the crate on the way home, and any noise that he makes. He will cry and wail for his mother, but it won't be long until you are home and able to comfort him, so just ignore the calls and concentrate on driving safely and getting him home in one piece. Once you arrive to pick up your puppy, it will all feel very exciting and go quickly. It's a good idea to take along your puppies new collar and ID tag and place it on him straight away once you get there. Remember to allow enough space between the collar and his neck, not too tight, not too loose. You don't need to leash him yet, you will most likely carry him out when you leave and that is perfectly fine.

The breeder will obviously be there when you collect your puppy, and you should use this to gain some pointers about your puppies behavior. They might not offer much, but in my experience, some breeders have said things like 'he loves to chew', or 'he hates being alone'. Although these might have been very general observations, they helped me be mindful of that particular puppy and keep an eye out and prevent certain behaviors in those early hours of bringing him home.

Another few things I would try to get from the breeder are:

- Paperwork (registration, purebred certificates, etc)
- Worming & Vaccination Schedule
- A blanket or item of clothing that smells like your puppies mother
- A small supply of the food he has been eating
- A toy or bowl, something that will be familiar to him

Ask the breeder where the puppies have been going to the toilet eg. grass yard, concrete, gravel, etc. This will help you find a spot that will feel familiar to him once you get home.

Load him up into his crate (which you have already prepared earlier!), and off you set. Take it easy on the drive home. Your puppy will not be used to traveling in a car, so be aware of this and try to take corners easy and not too fast. If you live far away, break the trip up into small trips, allowing him to get out and have some water and perhaps a potty stop along the way. If you are close by, just get there as quickly and as safely as possible.

You'll be home before you know it and you're ready to take him into his forever home!

Arriving Home - The Important First Day

This is very exciting for both you and your puppy. Keep in mind that he has just been taken away from all he has ever known... His mother, his siblings. So it will take some time for him to adopt his new 'pack'. You can make it easier for him by being there as much as possible in those first few days (I recommend taking time off work if possible, at least a week).

Once you get home, don't take him inside your house straight away. He will be exhausted from the drive home, and he might not have had the chance to go to the toilet yet, so take him to wherever you have decided he will go to the toilet. Remembering where he went when he was at the breeder's, try to take him to a similar spot for this first time at least. Allow him a few minutes to see if he will relieve himself, if he doesn't, don't stress too much. There will be plenty of new smells and sights going through his head, so don't worry too much at this point.

From there, take him to his new den. Place the blanket or item of clothing that has his mothers smell in there and put him down in there. Hopefully, you have some toys in there for him to chew on and plenty of comfy blankets. If you are planning on having him sleep in his crate, collect this from your car and place into his area.

You can now try and feed him a small meal, inside his new area. Allow him to eat and have a drink, and take him straight back out to see if he is ready to eliminate. Be sure to have your treats ready to reward him, the house training starts now.

If he is still wide awake and playful, by all means, have a play and some bonding time. Before you know it, he will be sleepy and it would be the perfect time to take him back inside to his den and his crate. Most puppies will only be awake for around an hour at a time, and will then sleep. They need lots of sleep, much like human babies, so allow for this and plan your schedule accordingly. Once he wakes, the first thing you need to do is to take him straight back outside, to let him go to the toilet.

The first day will fly by, and before you know it will all be over. He may cry throughout the night, and your way of approaching how to deal with this is your choice completely. Try to take him out to the bathroom before you set down for the night, and if he wakes you, take him out again and then put him back to his den.

The Remainder of the First Week At Home

This week will fly by. Try to take it all in, he will never be this small again. Take lots of photos, play with him and enjoy just how clumsy he is! There may be times when you get frustrated with him and don't expect him to take to housetraining right away. There will be accidents, but remind yourself it won't be forever. Don't forget to get your housetraining off to the right start, and don't relax on it.

Throughout your playtime during the week, you may have noticed some extra puppy proofing that needs to be done. We did go over some initial puppy proofing, but there are always some extra items that you just skip over or simply don't realize will be an issue until your puppy is digging his way under the fence!

Attend to these issues as quickly as you can. If you notice that you just aren't getting enough time to attend to them, or your list of puppy proofing just grows and grows, ask for some help from a friend or pay for someone to come by and help you patch up.

It's important that your yard is safe, especially if you plan to leave him there when you eventually go back to work. You can section off part of your yard if there are just way too many issues to solve. You can also purchase outdoor dog runs which may be a viable option, although I would recommend this only be temporary (depending on the breed, of course).

Communicating With Your Puppy

One thing I also like you to work on in the early days is how to speak to your puppy. Good communication is key to any relationship that you will have in your life, and the relationship with your puppy is no different.

Your puppy is not a mind-reader, so learn the language of your dog, and try to get good at it very early on. Dogs cannot speak as such, although they will bark and whine. The main type of communication your dog will use with you is their body language. This could include wagging their tail, crouching down to the ground, putting their tail between their legs, pricking their ears up to listen, fur standing upright on their back, moaning when you scratch his ears, sitting with mouth slightly open and panting, standing over another individual (another pet or human), etc.

You see, there are so many different ways that your dog will communicate with you. Try to take in as much as you can and study what your puppy does and why he is doing it. It might help to write things down and see if any patterns develop.

Some things that you should be aware of when you are communicating with him are:

- Standing over your puppy - You will be much taller than him and this can be frightening and intimidating to him. Allow him to approach you and try to make yourself smaller by kneeling down to a more reasonable size.
- Avoid eye contact for too long - Some eye contact is ok, and since you are the master, you should make eye contact with him. However, don't stare at him as this makes dogs feel threatened and it might cause him to become anxious or even aggressive.
- Hugging and Kissing - I would try to avoid these, at least for a few days. At least until you know what makes your puppy upset, and what he likes. Many dog bites happen because a human has tried to kiss the dog and he has mistaken this for an aggressive movement towards his

face (a kiss is a human affection attribute, not a dog one).

When approaching a new dog, I always try to offer my hand out for them to sniff me first. Think about it, how do dogs greet each other? They sniff each other. So, let him do that to you too. Once he seems comfortable with that, proceed to offer a scratch around his chest area or his neck. Avoid the top of the head, and most certainly don't slap the top of his head like many people think dogs like.

While communicating with your dog, you can still remain 'the boss'. You can be kind to him, but also be respected by him. You can use your voice in a calm tone and use short phrases. If he begins to take advantage of you, stand up slightly, and show him that you are bigger than him. Use this with caution though, you do not want to threaten him, or things may take a turn for the worse. If all else fails, simply get up and walk away for a second. Then approach a short time after, offering your hand again and start over.

Also worth noting, is that puppies have a tendency to 'pretend'. During play, they might sound aggressive, or pretend to be submissive to lull you into playing with them. A good way to tell what his true feelings are in this circumstance is to visually break his body down into pieces. Look at his front half, where he might be growling and barking towards you... Now, look towards his back end. Is he wagging his tail or bottom? More often than not, the puppies tail will be a dead giveaway as to how playful he is being, just remember in this scenario, that you are the master and you decide how aggressive he can be during playtime. If he starts to take it too far, give him a gentle telling off, and if it continues become firmer until he starts to play more gently.

Insider tip: When playing with a puppy, pretend to sneeze! Dog's sneeze when they play to show you they are only playing and it's nothing too serious!

Housetraining

I've mentioned this in this chapter because it is probably the most important thing you can do to help life within your home stay pleasant in the first few weeks. However, I go into detail about this process later in the book, so keep reading ahead and we will come back to this.

Bonding With Your New Puppy

The first weeks at home with your puppy are a special time, for both of you. You will be making a new friendship, and your puppy will be enjoying every single ounce of attention that you are giving him.

You will be spending a lot of time with your pup in the first few days of his new life at home with you. You will be the one who gets to introduce him to your home, the people in it and the places that he can now call his own. You are his pack now, and he will feel welcome if you let him.

It is important to spend time bonding with your puppy. If you can spend enough time with him in the first few days (again, try to take time off work so you don't have to leave him), you will develop a great relationship straight away. I am a huge believer in the bond you create with your puppy. The bond you develop through the time you spend with him, will make many things easier, including training him. This is because he will trust you, listen to you, and most importantly, he will respect you. He will look up to you and admire you... there is no greater love than that of a dog to his master.

If you are struggling to find things to do with your puppy to help your bond, try these following things:

- Communicate effectively - remember to speak to him in a kind voice, show respect to him, but also authority. Don't be shy, some people feel silly talking to dogs because they don't talk back. But watch his body language and you will see he does talk back, just in dog talk.
- Lead by example - Dogs learn by watching more than listening. Take the lead and do what you want him to do. Use physical actions more than vocal ones, a combination of both is perfect.
- Train your puppy, every day! - This is one of the most effective bonding experiences. He will learn to listen to you and respect you. All while learning and becoming a better companion. The perfect balance.
- Playing games - Get down on the floor and roll around with him! Let him chew and play tug-of-war with him. Wrestle, play fetch... Let him

have fun and be there when he is having fun!

- Stay Calm - Most important when you are training him, but also in everyday activities. If you yell at your puppy, he will get scared and this will hurt your relationship. Like with human babies, sometimes it's better to close the door and take a few deep breaths, then deal with the problem. Stay calm, and don't yell or scream at him.
- Take him out to run errands - The small things matter to your puppy. You are his world, so take him out with you and let him experience your life with you. This could be as simple as a car ride to the shop, he will love it and love you for letting him in on your life.
- Make walks fun and meaningful - Daily walks are a great bonding session. Make it even more eventful by trying some small training routines within the walk itself. Make him sit before the road, before you let him off the leash, make him stay when birds are near. Let him listen to you, and reward his good behavior. This will show you are not only in charge but also fun, no matter where you are.
- Tell him you love him - Dogs understand you. Don't underestimate that. Give him a cuddle before bed, give him a kiss when you get home. Lay on the floor with him, and pat him while the TV is on. Speak to him and say 'Love you!'. He will understand, and he will return the love.

- BASIC COMMANDS -

YOUR PUPPIES FIRST TRAINING SESSION

Finally! We have made it all the way to training day, and now that you have picked your breed, established the rules, prepared your home, and of course your little ball of fluff is home with you, it's time to get training!

It is important to start training right away. Do not give your puppy free rein of the house for a few days, because this is where bad habits start to form. They start early and even just one day can cause huge setbacks. One day in a puppy's life is a long time, and because they learn so quickly, it is imperative to take advantage of that sponge like brain.

In this chapter, we will go over the basic commands that you should start out teaching your puppy. These are the most useful commands, and the bare minimum you should be teaching your dog. These commands alone will get you an obedient dog and one worth showing off. These commands will also provide a cornerstone for future commands as you will find out later in this book.

Okay! You're ready, the puppy is ready...

Let's begin training!

First Things First

You have taken the big first step and you are about to start training your cute puppy. Here is what I suggest you do to help your first (and future) training sessions go off without a hitch.

- Treats - Dogs love treats! But, each dog is different and you will have plenty of time to experiment. Your dog might like deli meats, or cold sausages... Whatever it is, find out what drives them crazy and use it in your training sessions. If they like their treats, they will be more likely to listen and obey your commands. Make sure the treats are small, bite-sized and can be consumed within a second or two is ideal. Try to get something that doesn't require lots of chewing, but even their everyday kibble will be fine.
- Positivity - It is key in your training that you stay calm and keep your chin up. At times, it will get difficult. However, the moment you get down on your training and give up, your dog will pick up on your vibes and do the exact same thing. A tip I like to give; When you get frustrated, try again. When they finally get it, go nuts! Pat them and give them all the praise in the world and even a bonus treat or two! (sometimes I roll around on the ground with them, they love it!) This will go so far in improving their behavior. Once you're done celebrating that one triumph, do it again. Immediately! Dogs will pick up on your emotions, so stay positive, you'll get there through perseverance.
- Praise is the biggest reward for your puppy. At times, it will be more beneficial to them than the treat you are offering. Don't ever forget to praise your dog, or they will lose faith and not bother listening to you.
- Find a place to do your training every day. If you don't have a yard big enough, you might need to find somewhere else to take your puppy to train. Most of the basics you will learn shortly will be ok in a small yard, but as you and your puppy progress, you might find you start to run out of space. Take your puppy to the same place for training every day. Try not to confuse them too much and at the same time, try not to make the venue stimulating either. You want their sole focus on you

(and the treats!), not their surroundings.

- The final tip before we get started is for right at the beginning stages of your training. Your puppy is likely to be very small... so get down to his level. In doing this, you won't be anywhere near as intimidating for them. You don't need to be at eye level, always be the master. But reducing the impact of your size can help greatly, especially at the beginning of your training days.

Once you have these few things worked out, we can begin.

Watch Me - The First Command

This command is what I like to teach first. Although not essential for obedience, I see it as an important step for a puppy. Their attention span is so short that getting their focus for a few seconds could be the difference between a successful training session and failure.
Down the track, it can become useful when trying to divert their attention from something, whether it be another dog or a cat that has jumped into your yard.
You may not need an actual name for this command as simply saying their name will get their attention. This exercise in itself is a great way to teach your new puppy their name.

Here is a simple way to practice:

1. Get a treat in your hand and sit in front of your puppy.
2. Say their name (or if using a command say that). If they look up to your face, give them the treat.
3. If they don't look up at you, wave the treat in front of their eyes and move it towards your face. Once they look at your face, say the command and offer the treat.

This shouldn't take too long for most puppies, and once your pup has the hand of it, move forward to the next command.

Sit

This is the most basic of all the dog commands. Whilst being the most basic, it is very much the most important.

It is very cute to see your dog sit on command, look up at you with their gorgeous little eyes and wait for your next instruction. Or it might simply be a way of getting them to wait for a big pat or ready to throw that stick one more time. Not only this, but it can also become crucial, potentially saving your pooch from running onto a busy road or jumping all over an elderly person, knocking them down and injuring them - nobody wants that.

Here is my preferred way to teach the 'Sit' command:

1. While standing slightly higher than your puppy (get down on your knees if you need to get slightly lower) hold a treat just above their nose.
2. Gradually move the treat back over their nose, towards their eyes.
3. As you do this slowly, he should begin to lower his backside towards the ground.
4. Command 'Sit!' Be sure to use a firm, loud and clear voice.
5. If he struggles to hit the ground with his backside, you can gently touch the top of his back, near his bottom to assist him putting it down firmly on the ground.
6. As soon as his backside touches the ground, give him the treat and a huge amount of praise. Make a big fuss the first few times, this will give him a heap of encouragement.

Lie Down (Or 'Lay')

This is a great command to follow on from the initial command of 'Sit'. As your puppy will be sitting already, it is an easy follow on to get them to 'Lay'. Although many see this as a non-essential command, I think it is only a few extra steps added to the sit training, and see it worth your while to add this to your pups repertoire.

It may come in useful when you are sitting at a park bench and your dog just wants to get up and go. If they are in a *sit* position, it is easy for them to do that, whereas if they are laying down completely, it requires much more effort on their behalf.

It is also a useful position for your dog to be in if you wish to teach them further 'tricks', such as 'roll over' or 'Bang!'.

Many puppies will also go to this position naturally as they tire during your training session. After a few *sits*, they will get tired so once you see them beginning to *lie down*, say it out loud, and reward them when they hit the ground. They will soon learn the command and you haven't had to do much to teach them this additional command.

If they need some extra encouragement to *lie down*, this is my preferred way to help them learn:

1. If your puppy isn't already in the 'sit' position, follow the above steps to get them there.
2. Once there, get a new treat and hold in your hand, hide it and allow your puppy to smell it.
3. Once their nose is sniffing at your hand, lower it down towards the ground and speak out your command. 'Lay' 'Lie Down', say it loud and clear.
4. Your puppy should follow your hand, so begin to move your hand backwards, towards your body along the ground. Do this until his whole underbody is touching the ground.
5. Reward him once he touches the ground and of course, give a lot of praise.
6. Where possible, try to get him to stay in that position for a short

amount of time. You can do this by not standing straight back up yourself, and also placing a few treats in front of him so he stays laying for a few seconds.

Stay

A very important command to teach your pooch, at the top of the list with *sit*. Teaching your puppy to stay on demand will teach them to obey your call and wait for you to decide what they do next. There may be situations where this will come in handy, walking in the park or if visitors come to the side gate and you don't want your large dog to bounce all over them.
A word of warning for the 'stay' command: Puppies are just as impatient as humans. With this exercise, you will need to start small. Try to get them to stay while you take one step back, then return and give a treat. Next, go two steps back. And return. Do this over and over as you get farther and farther away. Don't take it too far though, they will lose interest and wander off once they're bored.
Now that you have both the *sit* and *lie* commands down, you can teach *'Stay'* in both of those positions.

Follow this procedure:

1. If your puppy isn't already sitting or laying down, follow the above steps to get them there.
2. Decide on a hand signal to show the dog for this command, I use a flat palmed hand. Tell them to 'Stay!', using a firm voice and showing them your hand signal.
3. Take a step back. If he stays, return to him and reward him with a treat and big praise.
4. Do it again, this time though, take two steps back. If he stays, return and reward again, being sure to give more praise than the first time.

One other note on this command: This is the first time I have mentioned using a hand signal. There may be instances when this is more useful than the vocal command. For example, you are in an area with lots of people around and can't yell out for whatever reason. So your dog looks at you, you use your hand signal and say the command normally (they will likely still hear you, the power of the dogs hearing and all!) and because you have trained them so well, they will know to stay there.

You can use hand signals for all commands, however, some are more important than others.

Recall (or 'Come', 'Here' etc)

Firstly, choose which command name you will use. Pick one and stick to it. I use *Come*, but only because that's what my mother used for our dogs! I know plenty of people who use the command *'here'* and that is fine too.
Again, an absolutely imperative command to teach your puppy. If you plan to walk your dog off-leash, this command is probably more important than sit or stay.
The ability to have your dog return back to you in an instant is so important in countless situations. Here's one:
You're out walking your German Shepherd. He's off leash in the dog park and you're by yourself. You know that he doesn't like small dogs, but you haven't seen any other dog's around, so all is well. You turn the corner and BOOM! Small dog! But wait, where is your dog? You command him to *'Come'* and he returns to your side, like the good boy you have trained him to be. (Oh, by the way, please always keep your dog in your vision, that's something I'll touch on later)
If you hadn't taught your puppy to *come*, this example could have ended in your dog pouncing on another dog, injuring it badly. We don't want that for any dog, no matter the shape or size of them.

So this is how to avoid it:

1. If your puppy isn't already sitting or laying down, follow the above steps to get them there.
2. Use the 'stay' command to get your puppy to sit away from you, a few steps is fine to start with.
3. Instead of returning to him, call out *'Come!'* in a loud and clear voice.
4. Hold a treat in your hand with your arm outstretched towards him and gesture back towards your chest.
5. Once he reaches you give him the treat straight away and give him lots of praise.
6. Repeat the steps, getting a little bit farther away each time.
7. After a few training sessions, catch him by surprise one day in the

yard. Wait until he is distracted, and shout *'Come!'*. If he obeys your command be sure to reward him with a treat and the biggest praise you've ever done. Don't worry if he ignores you, just keep training and it will come. (Try not to stand there shouting the command over and over when trying to catch him out, this will only teach him to disobey that command. Try saying it once or twice, if he doesn't respond, try again later.)

If you are having trouble with this command, try putting his leash over his head and take a step back. If he doesn't *'come'*, tug on the leash a bit and say the command out loud while tugging gently. Try this a few times, and once he gets it, take the leash off and try again.

A side note for this command would also: Try to introduce a hand signal once you are getting further away from him. This may be a simple pull back of your hand to your chest, or some people like to throw their hands above their heads (like a Mexican Wave). This helps when you are out walking in the dog park and they can see your command, they will recognize it and hopefully return to your side.

Go To Bed

Although not a 'must-teach- command, I have found this is one of the most used commands. You might not train this one at the same time as you will the others, as it will likely be used in different scenarios.

You can however, adopt the same principles of praising, rewarding and using your patience to teach this to your dog.

It will be helpful if you have nailed down the sit and stay commands, but in teaching *Go To Bed* to your puppy, it might help reinforce those commands also. Pick a place in the house you would like them to go when you need a bit of space, or when visitors come to the door, or perhaps where you would like them to sleep. It might be helpful to put a mat down or just their doggy bed will be fine - this helps them distinguish where they need to go.

Then, try these steps:

1. Get close to your puppy and use your command. Eg *Got to bed! Bed! Mat!*
2. Lure him over towards the bed with a treat if he doesn't move there himself.
3. To begin with, as soon as he touches the bed, reward him and praise him.
4. Next, take him off the bed and do it again. This time, wait until all 4 paws are on the bed.
5. Reward him, with more praise.
6. While still standing on the bed, ask him to '*Lay*' (or whatever command you used above for laying down).
7. Once his belly touches the bed, reward him.

After he has grasped the concept of '*Go To Bed*', you can start using the *Stay* command to help him understand to remain laying on the bed. If he steps off, that is fine. Just do the process over again and get him to stay there. Start out small, allowing him 10 seconds on the bed, then 20 seconds. Work your way up, small amounts each day. He will get there, I promise.

You can then move this to different rooms. If you're planning to have your puppy in with you of a night, then start the training over again in your bedroom. He won't take as long once he understands the commands, but it helps him understand if you go through the process again.

- ADVANCED TRAINING COMMANDS -

BECOMING AN OUTSTANDING CANINE CITIZEN!

Now that we have gone over the basic commands and you have a good understanding of what it will take, I can start showing some more advanced commands.

Some of these aren't 'commands' as such. Some are more along the lines of general obedience, such as walking on a leash and walking to heel. These will take time for you to learn, especially if you have never tried teaching a dog these techniques before.

Everyone is different, so you need to find your preferences. For example, the correct way for a dog to walk on a leash is for them to be slightly behind you. You are the master, therefore you lead him.
However! Not everyone does it this way, some like the dog to be ahead of them for different reasons. So, it is up to you how you wish to teach your puppy, use the below descriptions as a simple guideline.

I would recommend trying to get a grasp on the above commands first. They don't need to be perfect, but if your pup has a general understanding of the sit, lie, stay routine, then that will go a long way when you venture out on long walks.

Collar & Leash

If you haven't already, get your puppy used to wearing his leash. It's not natural for a puppy to wear a leash, nor a collar. After a while, it will of course become normal for them. But it might take a little while, some puppies longer than others. If you plan to have a collar on your puppy at all times (I would highly recommend this), then simply put one on him from as early as possible.

You need to be careful they don't catch on anything, so a properly fitted collar is important. The collar should be lightweight, and flat. No studs or ribbed collars for little pups!

If he takes to it right away, brilliant. If he seems uncomfortable or it is making him stressed, take baby steps. Put it on for a few minutes, then take it off. Put it on again a short while later, this time for a little longer. Take it slowly and you will get there.

Many puppies will simply sit on their butt and not move once you attach the leash to their collar. This is fine to begin with and try not to pull on the leash too much as they will potentially struggle against you and choke themselves. For now, just get them wearing the leash without going anywhere. Take your time and remember to be positive and use plenty of treats!

One more thing you might want to consider is getting a harness, rather than attaching the leash to the collar of your puppy. A harness relieves the neck of the stress that is caused by the puppy pulling, and many trainers find it vastly improves the speed of which their pup takes to the leash. The puppies front legs will go through two legs holes on the harness which clips at the top of their back. You then attached the leash to the top where there will be a clip. Not only is it more friendly and humane (nothing worse than hearing a dog choking while walking), it will give you more control when your puppy begins pulling.

A little trick is to put the harness & leash on at meal time. Your puppy will be easily distracted by their food they will forget the collar or leash is on at all.

Leash Training

Now that you have your puppy used to wearing their collar and leash, it's time to begin walking with it. This is a crucial step in your obedience training and one that you will need to spend a big chunk of time perfecting.

In many countries around the world, it is the law that your dog needs to be on a leash when out in a public space. It is not only the law but by having your puppy on a leash, it will keep your puppy safe in the big wide world. It opens up so many different opportunities for your dog, who, once leash trained, can go everywhere with you.

They can go down to the store with you, to the beach with the family or even travel the country with you!

It is hard work, and it will take time. So let's get to it:

- Get your puppy to sit on your left side as you both face forward.
- Decide on a cue, such as 'Let's Go!', and begin walking.
- Hold a treat directly in front of his nose.
- Do not let your puppy jump up at the treat, if they are jumping at it, lower the treat.
- After 5-8 steps, stop and tell them to 'Sit!'.
- Reward them with the treat and praise them.
- Start over, commanding 'Let's Go!' again and repeat the steps, increasing the distance each time.

Adding in the 'Heel' command

If you plan to compete in dog trials or competitions, you will need to master this. If you don't plan on entering your puppy, then this isn't essential. Your puppy will need to be slightly behind you, making you the 'leader'. Don't let them drag along behind you though, it really is only a nose behind you, almost by your side.

For those who wish to have a well-mannered dog on the lead, I encourage you to do the following:

- Get your puppy to sit on your left-hand side as you both face forward.
- Command 'Let's Go!' and begin walking.
- Hold the leash steady in your hand and if he starts to pull, allow him to reach the end of the leash for saying 'Heel!' in a loud, firm voice.
- Gently correct him back to your left-hand side and reward with a treat.
- Do the same thing if he is falling behind you.

This will take a bit of getting used to for both of you but stick at it. Even if you don't intend to enter your dog into a competition but find you are struggling to control your dog on the leash, this would be worth spending a bit of time teaching. An example would be if a larger breed of dog is taking you for a walk, rather you walking him. If you get what I mean!

Remember, you are in charge. If he begins to pull, sometimes it's easier to stop and start over.

Advanced Sit

I like to call this command the 'Advanced Sit', simply because it is effectively a normal sit, but with a small difference. Essentially what you are going to teach is for your puppy to 'Wait'. I use the 'Wait' command for this, but you can choose your own cue if you don't want to use mine.

What you are teaching is for your puppy to wait for you if they are off in the distance (off lead).

For example, you are walking in the dog park and pooch is off in the trees sniffing around. You are walking 10-20 meters behind them and notice something in the trees you aren't sure about. So you shout your command, they sit and wait on the spot for you.

Another example would be if they are approaching a road and you aren't right next to them.

You are almost merging 'Sit' and 'Stay' into one command, and you can use it when they aren't directly by your side. Obviously, it is important they have the sit and stay command pretty well down before you try to teach this.

The most effective way to teach this command is:

- When you're at home bring your pet to a doorway that has the door closed.
- Tell him to 'Sit'.
- Open the door gently, and wait to see if he bolts out the door. If he makes a break for it, close it quickly before he gets out.
- Announce your 'Wait!' command and try again.
- Open the door gently and reward him for not moving, then let him out.
- As he runs out, use a release command, such as 'Ok!'. This lets him know it is ok to move again.
- Practice for a few days (or weeks) until trying it out in the backyard.

Once he is out in the yard and walking in front of you, trying saying 'Wait!' out loud. If he stops, quickly give him a treat and a big amount of praise.

Another way to get this command working is to use it for their meal times. Make them sit as you place their bowl on the ground, command 'Wait!' while they are sitting. Then give the release cue, 'Ok!' and they can begin eating.

As you can see, this will take a long time to perfect. It will have many uses around the home and in public. Start training this early and you will not regret this handy command.

Give (or 'Drop It')

This is a useful cue to teach, especially when your puppy is putting anything and everything into their mouth to chew! It will still remain handy later in their life. Perhaps when they pick something up on your walk in the park or when you are simply playing fetch in the backyard.

Most dogs grasp this command quickly, however, others try to play tug-of-war with you when you attempt to take something from them.

An easy trade-off is to offer a treat, like so:

- Give your puppy one of his favorite toys.
- Let him play for a minute or so.
- While he has the toy in his mouth, hold a treat up to his nose.
- If he releases the toy, give him the treat.
- Try again, a few times over.
- Now add the cue 'Give!', in a loud and clear voice. Offer a treat when he complies.
- After you feel like he is getting it, remove the treat and just offer praise and keep playing.

Teaching your puppy 'Give!' is a huge step forward to learning how to play 'Fetch!'

Quiet!

Teaching your dog to speak is a party trick and I thought about listing this in the Fun Tricks chapter of this book. The reason I decided to list it here is that this command can be used in many different ways, some for fun and others to stop bad habits, such as excessive barking.

As always have your treats ready. Keep them close by, or better yet, in your pocket. Decide on which cue you are going to use. I use 'Quiet!', but many others prefer to use Enough! or Hush!

Then, you will need to put your dog in a situation where he would normally bark. This might be someone knocking at the front door or the kids running around in the backyard. Whatever it is, be ready to be by his side with a treat in your hand as soon as the barking stops.

If he has a bark and growls for a few seconds (perhaps a dog is walking out the front), wait until he stops barking completely then reward him. Never give him a treat if he is still barking, or even if he is still growling. Wait until he is completely silent.

Once you have had the chance to practice this a few times, begin adding in your cue word. Do exactly the same thing... stand close by and have treats ready. Once he barks, wait and then as soon as he stops, use your command! Then give him the treat and a big pat.

- TRICKS & FUN TRAINING -

Owning a puppy isn't all about getting them to be super obedient all the time. Your cute companion deserves to have fun, as do you. You and your puppy should try to get into the habit of making training fun, this includes training the basics that we have already covered. Once you have some of those basics nailed down, it may be time to start teaching your puppy some fun tricks. This is fun for you, and because of the nature of the tricks, your puppy will enjoy them too.

Not only will he get rewarded for being a good boy and doing as he is told, but he will also get a treat and praise for rolling around on the ground. Or perhaps begging with his paws hanging ever so cutely in the air while he waits patiently for his reward.

These fun tricks are a great way to build on the basic commands you have already taught your puppy. It will help cement those commands and show your puppy why you have taught him these commands. You will see throughout this chapter that your puppy will need to know a few basic commands to learn the majority of the tricks.

Learning fun tricks is great mental stimulation for your puppy, and a great way to bond together in those early days at home. Puppies learn so quickly

that it is better to start these tricks when they are young. He will use his brain in different ways as well as teaching him to use different parts of his body, parts that he might not have used that much before.
I will go through some different tricks that you can teach your puppy, but the options for you are endless. Some dogs will do things that others wouldn't even attempt, so work out what your puppy likes to do and show him some tricks. The tricks I have in this book are what I would regard as the usual tricks you will come across as a dog owner. I don't delve into how to get your dog to surf, or how to teach your poodle to ride a skateboard.

Tricks are great to show off to your friends and help your puppy obey you while others are around!

Speak, Talk or Bark!

Teaching your dog to speak is a fun trick, and can be useful to scare away intruders or show off a pretend conversation between you and your dog to your friends. This trick can also be a cure for excessive barking as it teaches your puppy to only bark when you say it is ok!

It is helpful if your puppy already understands the 'Quiet!' command, meaning he stops barking when you tell him to. This is relatively easy to train, even though you have just read about it in the Advanced Training Techniques. If you skipped over the steps, I'd encourage you to track back and review them if you want to teach your puppy to speak on demand.

Once you have the quiet cue down, move forward to the next step.

As with most techniques, there are many different ways to teach this command, but my preferred method is the following:

1. Put your puppy in a situation where he is more inclined to bark. This might be getting someone to knock at the door so he barks.
2. As he barks, say your 'Speak' command, loudly and clearly.
3. Quickly give him a treat and a quick pat.

Keep repeating these steps, being sure to reward him every time he barks but only give him the treat if you used the 'Speak!' command.

After a while, try using the command somewhere else. You could be out in the yard, say 'Speak!' and if he barks then have your treat ready to go and praise him.

Shake Hands/Paws

Ah, the classic shake hands trick. Always a crowd favorite, no matter where your puppy might go. There is nothing more adorable than a little puppy offering his paw to a new person when they greet him, so be sure to get this one working as soon as possible!

This is the favorite trick for most dog owners, mainly due to the ease of teaching. It comes naturally to most puppies to raise their paws up in the 'Shake Paws' position so it is easy to teach and they tend to learn it very quickly as a result.

At most, your puppy should be shaking paws on command after only one or two training sessions. The only thing your puppy will need to have learned already is the 'Sit!' command.

Get him into this position and then try the following steps:

1. Holding the treat in one hand, wave the treat under his nose with a clenched fist.
2. Use your command, 'Shake!'
3. Most dogs will sniff your hand at first, and when they can't get to the treat they will start to paw at your hand.
4. As soon as he touches your hand with his paw, open your fist and reward him with the treat and a pat.
5. Keeping practicing the same methods for a few minutes at a time.
6. Once he begins to get it, remove the treat from the hand you want him to shake. Use your cue 'Shake!' and once he obliges, reward him with a treat from the other hand. (if he gets confused, start over and put the treat back in the original hand)

The best way to 'proof' this trick is to ask one of your friends to try to trick with your puppy. Be sure that they have a treat that they can reward your puppy with in the case that he completes the command for them.

Spin, Twirl or Round!

A really fun trick for your puppy. You will almost see the smile on his face and in his eyes when he starts to get the hang of this trick. This is another pretty basic trick that you can teach your puppy, but you can also make it more complex by throwing in which direction you want him to turn ie 'Left!' or 'Right!'.

The best part about this trick is that they can start learning right away with no basic commands really required to get started. So long as he is standing on all 4 paws, and you have his undivided attention, you're good to go.

Try following these steps:

1. With your puppy standing in front of you, hold a treat in front of his nose.
2. Slowly move the treat to one side of his head, enough so he has to move his head to follow it.
3. Once you move the treat in a full circle around his body, and he follows you and completes a full 'spin' give him the treat and use your cue (Spin, Twirl or Round).
4. Repeat the steps a few times, enough so he understands the action.
5. After a few training sessions, you can add in the direction. Only do this if he is getting good at the trick with the normal command.
6. To add the direction, use the above steps and instead of the normal cue, use the direction that you want him to go.
7. After a while, test him out by doing a combination of the directions eg Right! Right! Left! Right!

One thing to be aware of with this trick is that dogs do get dizzy, the same as you and I. Try not to train this trick for too long, or he will become confused and very dizzy. Try to teach this trick in small bursts or 1-2 minute sessions only.

Beg or Sit Pretty!

A very cute dog trick, beg is up there with the most popular tricks to teach. It is relatively easy for most dogs to learn too, and provides them with a chance to work on their balance skills when they are small pups.

Some owners don't like the command 'Beg', because they don't like the idea of their dog to be 'begging'. This is your choice, but one option to change the command could be to use 'Sit Pretty!'... Whatever command you decide to use, be sure it is quick and precise.

Your puppy will need to know the 'Sit!' command, but this is relatively easy to teach and teaching 'Beg!' can help cement the sit command into your puppy's brain.

My method for teaching 'Beg!' is as follows:

1. Have your dog in the 'Sit' position.
2. Hold a treat above his nose and use your command 'Beg!' (or whatever you choose to use)
3. Slowly raise the treat back over his head, holding it slightly out of his reach. Keep moving back until his front paws leave the floor.
4. To begin with, reward him for taking his paws off the ground. Eventually, you will want him to go further back so his front paws hang cutely in front of him.

As you advance with this trick, begin to just voice the command without holding the treat above his head. This may take a while, but with patience, he will get there. Use your command and show him the treat and in time he will go into the beg position naturally.

Roll Over!

Simply a classic dog trick. For good reason too, just like seeing your puppies eyes light up when doing a twirl, his eyes will light up as he rolls over on the floor ready for your next command.

This is slightly more difficult than the other commands that we have gone through so far, but can easily be broken down in steps. Your puppy would benefit from knowing sit and lie down commands, however, you can always try this command whenever he is laying down.

This is my method, which is straightforward and breaks down the steps to make it easier on your pooch.

1. Get your puppy laying down on his stomach.
2. Hold a treat to his nose and move it towards his shoulder.
3. Once he turns his head, give him the treat.
4. Do this a few times, and reward him each time he turns his head.
5. Repeat the above steps, but start getting him to lay on his side and then give him the treat.
6. Once he is on his side, it is pretty easy to get him to roll over. Simply hold the treat above his nose and he will use his momentum to take him the whole way over to the other side of his body. It is at this stage that you start using the command 'Roll Over'.

Soon enough you will have a puppy who is rolling over in front of you, and then looking up at you waiting for his reward.

If you are having trouble with your puppy jumping up after he completes his roll, try to slow the process down. A good way to do this is to hold the treat in front of his nose and move it slower as he rolls. If you move the treat too quickly, he will follow it and then momentum will speed him up, resulting in him jumping up after completing the move.

Bow! or Take a bow!

Getting your puppy to take a bow after showing off all of his other tricks, this is something you would see in the circus! Lots of dogs bow to each other, it is a natural body language movement of the canine. They are showing whoever is nearby that they are in the mood to play.

However, you can train your puppy to use this adorable trick in another way. A pooch who can bow on cue is bound to get a round of applause after his performance.

If your puppy already knows to sit and stay, this is the perfect trick to teach them.

Ideally, you want your puppy to be slightly touching the ground with his chest and his rear end will still be up in the air.

1. Get your puppy standing up and paying attention.
2. Hold a treat to your puppies nose and slowly lower it to the ground.
3. He will follow the treat so lure him down to the point where his 'elbows' are touching the ground.
4. After a slight pause get him to return to the standing position by moving the treat back up. Reward him with the treat and lots of praise.
5. Once he grasps the action, begin adding your cue word (Bow!).
6. Increase the amount of time you get him to pause in the bowing position by holding the treat to the ground and then returning him to the standing up position.

This trick may take some time because he will try to lay down at first. Break it down slowly for him and it's important not to pause for too long to begin with. Take it slowly for him and he will get the difference between the two commands 'Bow!' and 'Lie Down' eventually.

Play Dead! or Bang!

Playing dead is a great party trick for your dog to learn. It is a little more advanced than some of the other tricks I have explained so far but still fairly easy to teach if he knows a few of the basic commands already.

He will need to know the 'Lie Down' command already, so try to have that perfected before trying this trick. If your puppy knows the Roll Over trick mentioned above, then you won't have any trouble teaching this trick.

1. Get your puppy in a laying down position.
2. Hold a treat to his nose.
3. Move the treat to one side so that he will roll over to get the treat.
4. Once he reaches his back reward him and add your cue 'Dead!' or 'Bang!'
5. It will help the effect of the trick if you add a hand signal for the command (such as holding your hand in the shape of a gun)

You can have all sorts of fun with this trick. Many people like to add sentences, for example 'Would you rather be a cat, or would you rather be Dead!?'. Once your puppy hears the vocal cue and you use your hand signal on the word 'dead', he will lay down on his back... Very cute and very funny.

Kisses!

This isn't for everyone (personally I love it!), but a great trick nonetheless. Getting your puppy to show a human affection trait is adorable. He will love the attention it gives and when he hears your giggle or laugh it will make his day.

Rather than the usual treat of sausage or whatever you normally use, I find using a spread from the kitchen is easier. Something like peanut butter is perfect for this trick. Simply spread a small amount on your cheek and follow these steps to get him giving you big kisses on command:

1. Have a small amount of peanut butter on your cheek.
2. Use your vocal cue 'Kisses!'.
3. Lean towards him and he will lick the spread off your cheek.
4. He will be super keen to lick the treat from your cheek and it doesn't hurt to add another vocal cue to help him along.

Some puppies will get carried away with this trick, simply because they can't give enough love to their masters! In this case, it's a good idea to try and add another cue like 'Stop!' or 'Enough!' to get him to stop. Do this by using the finishing cue and waiting for him to stop licking you then reward him with a treat from your hand.

Although this is a very cute command to teach, not everyone appreciates being slobbered on by a dog. It is important to teach your dog restraint with this trick and don't let him get carried away, going around giving everyone kisses. One way to avoid all your guests getting slobbered on is to teach your dog to kiss your hand instead of your face.

Wave, Say Hello or Wave Bye

Now, we have already taught your puppy to bow, a sure way to impress after showing off all of his tricks. What if he can wave as he leaves the stage? That's sure to impress, and is very achievable once he knows some basics commands such as sit.

Just like the Bang! command, teaching your dog to 'wave' is simply using another part of another trick. This time it is very similar to 'Shake Paws', all you are doing is getting him to raise his paw in the same manner and leave it there for a few seconds. It will help immensely if he knows 'Shake Paws' already, so perhaps try that first before getting your pup to learn this trick.

Once you have perfected 'Shake Paws' try following these steps:

1. Give your puppy the 'Shake Paws' command.
2. When he lifts his paw to shake your hand, move your hand up so he has to reach a bit higher for your hand.
3. When he moves it higher, reward him.
4. Try this a few times, and once he gets his paw up high enough (so it looks like a wave), use your vocal cue and reward him.
5. Keep repeating this process and after a while, he will do it on command. Begin selecting only the good responses, meaning only treat him when he has his paw high enough.

Stand On His Hind Legs or Dance!

This might be difficult for the giant breeds of dogs, but if you start young enough, they might build up enough strength to do this properly. Getting your puppy to dance with you is very cute and something that you can enjoy together forever.

You can vary this however you want to... Adding in a twirl on his hind legs, or to slow dance with you cuddling him. The options are endless and you can pretty much choose how you would like him to dance with you.

My preferred method is pretty basic, and it will help if your puppy already knows the 'Sit' command.

1. Get your puppy in the 'Sit' position and focused on you.
2. Get a treat and hold it close to his nose.
3. Lift your hand over his head, slightly out of his reach so he has to reach up (hold it higher than you do for the 'Beg' command, he needs to get up higher for this trick).
4. Once he reaches his hind legs, add your vocal cue and reward him with the treat.
5. Repeat the process but now extend the amount of time he spends on his hind legs before you give him the treat.
6. Add in your trick at this stage if you wish. If you want him to complete a spin, simply hold the treat and lead him around in a circle with the treat. Take this step very slowly.

High Five and High Ten

If your dog does something very cool, how about being able to give him a high five? Or, you've made a classic joke and no one will give you a high five... but your best friend will give you one if you train him too. Never be left hanging again!

A fun trick that can be taught very easily following on from the 'Shake Paws' command. This command is very similar to the wave command, and there is no reason you can't have your puppy doing all three of these commands very quickly. Get him to learn the basic command of 'Sit' first and you're good to go.

Get your puppy into the 'Sit' position and focused firmly on you.

1. Use the 'Shake Paws' command to get him to lift his paw.
2. Hold your palm out, but in a high five position rather than the shakes paws position.
3. Once he touches your hand, use your vocal cue of High Five! and reward him.
4. After he understands what to do, use the other hand and get him to repeat the process (this gets him used to lifting both paws).
5. Now, to get him to 'High Ten', hold two treats in each hand and use the vocal cue of 'High Five'.
6. Once he touches both paws on both of your hands, use your new vocal cue of 'High Ten!' and reward him straight away.

High Five will be relatively straight forward if you have already mastered the 'Shake Paws' command, however the 'High Ten' command might take a little bit of getting used to for your puppy. Give him time though, and take it slow. If he isn't getting it right away, leave it for a day or two, and then try again. He will have to build a bit of strength to get this trick down, so take it easy.

- OBEDIENCE SCHOOL -

YES OR NO?

This is a prevalent question for many new dog owners, and although there is no blanket answer, I wanted to touch on it briefly in this book. I feel it is a very important topic, along with everything else in this book, so just a quick outline of the pros and cons of obedience school is the main aim of this brief chapter.

Many new puppy owners question the value of signing up to puppy school. The majority of us lead rushed lives, and to add another commitment can seem like one step too far. After all, you've just committed to spending more of your free time with your new puppy, training them, playing with them, walking them and housetraining them, and now you're expected to take them along to Obedience School, too!

I offer you to ask a few questions first of all, these may assist you in your decision in whether or not to pack your leash and treat bag and head off to Obedience School.

- Are you an experienced dog owner?
- Is this your first puppy?
- Have you trained a dog before? If yes, was that dog obedient?
- Have you had this type of dog before? (Think breed, size, energy levels...)
- What is the background of the puppy?

I think the first two questions are almost enough to answer whether you should attend a school or not. If you answer no to the first and yes to the second question, I would highly recommend going to at least a few puppy classes. Not so much for the puppy, but for you!

Then, I would encourage you to think about the type of dog you have just welcomed into your family. This will assist in your decision-making. For example, a Labrador is relatively straightforward to train, even a beginner dog owner would be able to teach a Labrador the basic commands in this book quickly, simply due to their intelligence and eagerness to be trained. On the flip side, if you are a beginner dog owner and have just adopted a Chow Chow, this breed is renowned for being difficult to train. In this case, I would recommend taking your cute ball of fur along to a few obedience classes (at least a few!).

OKAY! Let's go to school!

If you have decided to enroll your puppy in school, then I recommend starting early. This is something you can anticipate before your puppy gets home. Book ahead, as you may need to try a few different schools to ensure their schedule fits in with yours, and also whether they have any vacancies available to assist in your training.

The ideal age to start would be between 8 - 12 weeks of age. However, lots of puppies don't start until they are 6 months old, so this is completely your decision. Try not to wait too long, or wait until you are getting frustrated with your at-home training schedule because this will allow your puppy to form some bad habits right from the start.

Attempt to make a decision at the same time as when you decide to get your puppy, this will save any frustrations down the track.

Once you start Obedience School, you can expect to gain valuable on-hand tips, such as those outlined so far in this book. Many of the basics will be covered, things like sit, stay, lie down and how to walk on a leash. These are things covered in this book, but it might help you to get another trainer to look over you while you train your puppy, and offer tips and advice to how you can improve. Most schedules range from a 7 - 10-week training schedule, with the classes normally an hour in length once a week.

Another important aspect which taking your pup to school is the socialization aspect. There will likely be many other dogs at your Obedience School, and this is crucial in exposing your puppy to these elements that they will come across in their lives.

Don't expect Obedience School to solve issues such as barking, destructive behavior (chewing furniture, destroying gardens, etc) or anxiety from your puppy. These are things you can work on at home through different training methods, or if it doesn't seem to be getting any better, then seeing a veterinarian or animal behaviorist.

Which Obedience School do I go to?

Just like human schools, some puppy schools are better than others. This is a natural thing in all aspects of life, but I would recommend asking as one of your visits to the veterinary clinic. It is highly likely that they will know of a local or nearby school for your pup to attend, and many clinics actually offer Obedience Schools these days!

Some things to keep in mind when choosing which school to go to:

- Are the trainers certified trainers? Ask for proof.
- How long has the school been around for?
- Is it run to a professional standard? Are they friendly and actually good with the animals?
- Are you the one training, or does someone else do it? (please always choose a school where you are the master!)

I have full confidence that if you follow the steps in this book and take your puppy to at least one term of puppy school, you and your puppy will be well on the way to being happy and well-trained together, for a very long time.

- SOCIALIZATION -

TEACHING YOUR PUPPY TO GET ALONG WITH EVERYONE

The first few weeks of a puppies life are significant for many reasons. Many of which we have already covered, but socializing your puppy feels like the most important aspect in general terms of how well-mannered your grown up dog will be. The more exposure you are able to provide in those early weeks, the better they will be able to tolerate different environments and different people. By exposing them early on, your puppy will be able to remain calm and learn to accept the situations from a very early age.

Don't be mistaken though, there isn't a set amount of time that is determined that dictates when your puppy will be well-behaved in public. Like all the training we are doing in this book, it is the quality of the exposure that you give your puppy which will be most beneficial. Your puppy doesn't need to spend hours and hours with small children to be good with them. He will just need to right guidance and training when those particular circumstances arise. Like anything we have already gone through, he will also need a lot of praise when he does the correct things.

It is important to keep socializing fun, just like you should be doing with your training. Speak to him in the gentle tones we discussed early in this book, use treats to reward him and be there for him if he gets scared. If your puppy hesitates for some reason, allow him a second to assess the situation. Once he makes the move forward, walk beside him and reward his courage and willingness to explore.

If your puppy gets spooked in any new environments that you are exposing them to, don't force it upon them. Your puppy will grow and eventually things that scare him when he is young, won't be an issue in a few months time. Just take it slow, and support him. In my experience, forcing them to stay in one spot when they are clearly scared can seriously backfire, scarring the puppy for life.

For example, you take your puppy to the beach and you really want him to go for a swim. He touches the water and freaks out and runs back to you. Try taking him back to the edge of the water and offer a treat when the water touches his paws, if he freaks out again, just leave it for the day. And try again next time.

Unfortunately, sometimes circumstances beyond these owners control could have dictated their dog's lives before they became the owner of that particular dog. A common case when adopting dogs from the pound or Dogs Home. This is one advantage that you are going to have by getting your puppy when they are so young, you will have all the time in the world to help break any bad trauma they may have suffered already.

So, let's break it down a bit more so you can understand exactly what to do, when to do it and why to do it:

When should you start socializing your puppy?

The most ideal time to get started on your pups social skills is when they are between 8 - 16 weeks old. You might be thinking 'Oh, eight weeks old? I thought you said early!' While you would be correct in thinking this, the likelihood of you having your puppy before they are 8 weeks old is low, if you remember back to when we discussed when you will get your puppy at home (pups should stay with their mother's until at least 8 weeks of age).

Be mindful of your puppies vaccinations when starting to expose him to all the different situations that life will bring to him. Try not to take him somewhere where you aren't sure if all the other dogs are up to date with their vaccinations. This will put him at risk of various diseases and can be easily avoided.

You should never stop exposing your puppy to new things. This type of training will go well beyond their puppy years, as they grow so will their behaviors to different circumstances. You should aim to provide new people, new places, new dogs for your dog to meet for the remainder of their life, just to help cement their well-mannered social skills.

How to expose your puppy to all the different social aspects life brings?

You can start by simply inviting friends around to your home and introduce your puppy to them. It helps if you have friends of different sizes, ethnicities, different hair colors etc. Even if you have a friend who has facial hair, it will help your puppy learn to accept all different people into your home. When they come into your home, have treats ready and when he stays calm, reward him! Do all you can to stop him from jumping up. Ask your visitors to help you out by not showing him any attention when he does jump up.

After you have exposed him to different types of adults, try to bring some small children into your home. Be sure to keep an eye on small children, especially if they attempt to pull on your puppies tail (a common thing to happen with small children and dogs). It is easier to avoid situations like this by keeping a careful eye on what is happening in front of you. If your puppy has his tail pulled once or twice, he will quickly associate this pain with small children and that will not be good for future visitors with small kids. Puppies generally take well to small kids as they aren't as intimidating to them, but always keep a close eye over everything that is happening.

After exposing to different people, it might be time to try exposing him to different noises and smells. At home, try to make some loud banging noises every so often, it may startle him at first, but comfort him and show him it is ok by giving him a cuddle or a pat. Turn on the hairdryer and see how he reacts, some puppies love having the hot air blown in their fur... Try it out and reward positive behavior. However, if he doesn't like it, don't force it upon him. You can turn YouTube on and load a video of a loud truck, play it while he is around. This will aid you further when you head out of your house.

Once he is vaccinated, it would be wise to take him out beyond the boundaries of your home. If you can take him around your neighborhood, he might come across a loud car driving past, or someone mowing their lawns. These will likely be new noises to him, so great exposure to aid in his skills in the outside world.

You can also try walking him on different surfaces, as this may impact his routine and behaviors. Some puppies don't like walking on the gravel, so take him along there and watch his reaction. If he takes to it well, reward him. Then, take him to the beach. Does he like the feel of sand on his paws? If so, reward him.

Why is socialization so important?

The goal of this book is to help you have a well-trained, well-mannered dog.
Alongside obedience, the social skills of your dog are the most important part
of helping him become a happy and well-behaved part of your household.

Without helping him develop excellent social skills, your dog will be prone to
aggression and other behavior problems when they get older. If someone
approaches your property and your dog is socially inept, they may hurt the
person out of fear and anxiety. This would be due to lack of exposure as a
puppy, and something that you can help avoid.
It is a lot easier to train them early rather than trying to rid old habits that
have formed from when your grown-up dog was a puppy.

Some breeds are known to have more trouble adapting to certain aspects that
life will throw at them, so be aware of this too. If you know your puppies
parents, ask the breeder what their fears are, this may help you focus on
things to work on. The genetic makeup of your puppy will influence how
they react to different things, so it is well worth knowing the history of your
puppies family roots.

What if I am having trouble with socializing my pup?

If you are struggling to find different aspects to expose your puppy to, you can always take part in some dog training in your local area. A quick internet search should show plenty of options for you. Be aware though, your puppy will likely need to be vaccinated so this may not be available straight away.

There are always options, and below is a list of things you can do to help your puppy if you are running out of ideas:

- A simple walk around the block - you never know what, or who, you might run into!
- Visit the local mall - the different smells, sounds, and sights help your puppy adjust
- Strolling along a highway - the loud noises of trucks and speeding cars are important for your puppy to learn to ignore. Obviously, only do this where it is safe to do so.
- Playgrounds - exposure to small children is important, again use your brain with this and don't scare small kids away. Even walking the streets after school might be a good lesson for your puppy.
- Local Dog Park - great for exposure to different breeds of dogs, big and small.
- Visit the Vet - there will be many different animals there as well as a million different smells for him.
- Dog-friendly cafes - these are becoming more and more commonplace so use them to your advantage. Take plenty of treats, sit with a coffee and reward his good behavior.
- Take him to a friends house - new smells, new environment and perhaps even a new human to interact with. Make sure he's on his best behavior though!

- HOUSETRAINING YOUR PUPPY -

NO MESS INSIDE!

Ah... Finally. It has come to this. The dreaded housetraining... Most new puppy owners cringe at the thought of housetraining their new puppy. It has a bad name for being difficult, and to be honest, sometimes it can be.

Housetraining (or housebreaking, potty training whatever you choose to call it), is one of the first things that you will teach your puppy. You should begin housebreaking your puppy from the moment you take him home. Literally, the first thing you should do once you get him out of your car is to take him to the designated place you want him to relieve himself and wait for him to go.

I firmly believe in your ability to housetrain your puppy quickly, so much so that I am writing an entire book dedicated to the subject. It is aimed at helping you build a routine and get into the right habits right from the beginning. Consistency is key to housetraining, and this book will be based on a Monday - Sunday (7 days) schedule to help you achieve quick results.

Here is a link for the book newsletter which if you sign up, you will receive an email reminder when the book goes on sale. Just like this book, it will be available in ebook format as well as paperback.

<u>SIGN UP HERE!</u>

For now though, let's begin going over the basics of housetraining to give you a better understanding of what is going on and how you can help.

Things to remember

A puppy is of course, a newborn. You wouldn't expect much from a human baby in terms of toilet training, so you should adopt the same expectations for the early days of your puppies life at home with you.

A puppy will learn about toilet-time much quicker than a human baby though, so you can use this to your advantage. It is not uncommon for new pups to be housetrained within 7 days (that's right, 1 week!). I have done it, and so can you.

The biggest thing to remember is that accidents will happen. A puppy won't be able to control his bladder until around 12 weeks of age. Even if you stick to your schedule, and take your puppy out every 1-2 hours, accidents are bound to happen. It's important for me to stress to you that you don't punish him for these accidents. Do not ever rub his nose in it, this is an age-old technique that is cruel and achieves nothing other than teaching your puppy to fear you and fear going to the toilet. As a general rule, a puppy can hold its bladder for one hour per month old they are eg. 4 months old = 4 hours. This is a pretty general rule, and obviously has many varying factors such as how much water your puppy has had.

Another thing to remember is to try and stick to a routine. If you have taken a week off work as I suggested, this will be easier than if you are at work. Try to take him out at the same time every day, then also take him out after every meal, after every playtime, etc. You will essentially be taking him out after every activity that you do for those first few months.

If you find an accident in the house, do not punish your puppy after the fact. He will have forgotten what he has done by then, and by punishing him you will again just be teaching him to fear you. Simply clean the mess up and try to keep a closer eye on him in the future.

Watch for Signs

Puppies will show certain types of body language when they need to go to the bathroom. If you can learn very early on what his 'signs' are, then this will help achieve quicker results because you can see exactly when he needs to be taken out.

If you see him sniffing, circling around and pacing as if looking for something, it is a good idea to take him out. You should do so quickly, pick him up and take him straight out to his spot. It can be a matter of seconds between when he decides he needs to go and when he actually relieves himself.

If you catch him in the middle of the accident, firmly say 'No!'. Try not to startle him when you say it, this will scare your puppy. After saying your command, pick him up and take him straight out. In these circumstances, you might find that by the time you get him out there, he has finished (and you may also have wee all over your jumper now). This is normal, but by taking him out he will begin to associate the action he just did and where you have taken him and he will start putting the two together.

Choosing a command

Like with anything you are trying to teach your puppy you should try to add in a vocal command for him to learn. Toilet training is no different and you should try to think of something that you might like to use as his 'go on demand' signal.

This has many benefits, but none more so than when you have to take your puppy out when it is pouring with rain and you have to stand and wait for him to go. If you use your vocal command and he begins to learn what he is supposed to do when he hears that command, you can cut your time getting wet in the rain.

Try 'Go', 'Outside', 'Do Your Business' or 'Toilet'. Anything will work and for one of my dogs their command is 'Toi-Tois!' You really can say anything, so long as you are in the same spot every time and you reward his behavior. After saying your command, wait for him to go. Once he relieves himself, say the command once more and reward him with a treat. Try this every time you go out and you will soon have a puppy that goes on command.

You can also differentiate between wees and poos with your command. Simply use the same method, but change the vocal command and reward the difference in behavior.

Using a crate

If you are going out or you know you will be away from home, you should place your puppy in a crate. I can't stress the importance of this enough in terms of housetraining your puppy.

Dogs, by instinct, do not want to soil their territory. They are proud animals and most are relatively clean animals who do not like sitting or laying in their own waste.

You should get a crate if you wish to housetrain your puppy quickly, making sure that it is big enough for them to grow into. If it is too big when he first comes home, simply place a divider in there to shrink the space he can lay down in. The area available to him should be enough so that he can turn around but not too much more than that.

Every time you leave him you should place him into the crate. You can have a small amount of water in there, however not too much as this will make him want to go. Place his bed in there too, puppies will not go to the toilet where they sleep. Try not to leave him for any longer than 4 - 6 hours, this will be asking too much of him at the early stages of housetraining. If you need to go to work, try coming home and letting him out to the toilet in the middle of your day or ask someone who lives close by that you trust to come and let him out. Be sure they know where to take him in your yard, you can't afford for him to get confused about where to 'Go'.

You can choose not to crate train, but I find it is by far the best way to speed up housetraining your puppy. Some people prefer training pads set away from the puppies bed. Puppies prefer to go to the toilet on an absorbent material such as these pads (or grass) so they will be more inclined to go on these pads rather than the floor next to it.

Other Problems and Cleaning Up Accidents

Each dog are their own, and as like with babies, they will all learn at a different pace to each other. It is important for you to remain patient and even though I've stated that you can achieve a housetrained puppy in 7 days, you shouldn't get disheartened if this doesn't happen. Especially if you haven't housetrained a dog before!

It may take several months for your puppy to get the idea of going in the one spot that you have decided for him. If you notice he keeps gravitating to a different spot in the yard and he seems to prefer it there, then consider changing where you want him to go. He needs to be comfortable so keep this in mind.

This can be a long process but you will begin to see the results. It's common for you to think you have successfully taught him and that he is fully housetrained, only for him to turn around the next day and leave you a surprise in the laundry. This is normal, just go back and remain diligent with your attention and watch him like a hawk until you are completely confident he has it down.

When the inevitable happens and your puppy has an accident indoors, remember to clean it up as soon as possible. You will also need to use a cleaner that eliminates odors and give the spot a good scrub. If you avoid this step you puppy may pick up on the scent that his waste has left behind, and he will go in the same spot again.

If you are finding that your training doesn't seem to be working and you have allowed enough time (up to 4 months of age), it may be possible that there is an underlining health issue causing him problems controlling his bladder. This could be as simple as a urinary tract infection, or something more serious. Something to be aware of but again, allow enough time to housetrain your puppy before jumping to this conclusion.

- CLICKER TRAINING -

AN EFFECTIVE METHOD OF TRAINING

In the future, I plan to write an entire book dedicated to this subject because I firmly believe this is an effective way to train your puppy. Clicker training relies heavily on positive reinforcement for your puppy and doesn't use much negative behavior ie; yelling, taking away your attention, time outs, etc. I believe this is the best training method possible so I will touch on the subject briefly, but if you wish to learn more about clicker training then please keep an eye out for my future book.

Although I believe in clicker training, I still train without it sometimes and it works perfectly. Which is why I have written this book with only one chapter dedicated to clicker training. Not everyone uses it, and that is perfectly ok with me.

Ok, let's get into clicker training.

What is clicker training?

Clicker training is a popular training method for many dog owners. The term 'clicker' comes from the handheld item that the trainer holds in their hand. The trainer pushes a button on the item and it makes a short and sharp 'click' sound. There are many different types of clickers on the market, but let's be honest... Your dog won't care what you clicker looks like, or what color it is. So buy the cheapest one you find, I promise it will work perfectly fine.

The most important part of clicker training is that the trainer learns to time their clicks correctly. The idea is that you click at the exact moment that your dog does the behavior that you desire. For example, you command your dog to 'Sit!', and as soon as his bottom touches the ground you click and reward him with a treat.

You must always give your dog a treat whenever you click. This is rule number one for clicker training. If you miss giving a treat once, the clicker begins to lose some of its effectiveness. If you reward him with a treat each and every time he hears the click he begins to remember it is that he is doing when he hears the click. Having said all this, you don't have to always use a clicker when training. If you forget to take your clicker, or you seem to have lost it (or puppy had chewed it!), don't forego training just because you don't have it. You can still train, just use vocal praise instead of the clicker.

When should you click?

You don't have to be in 'training mode' to use your clicker. Try to get in the habit of taking your clicker with you wherever you go in the house. Make sure you have treats with you too, I always have treats in my left-hand pocket. If my dog sees me with my hand in my pocket he will do anything I ask him to do because he has learned over time that I have always got treats in there.

By carrying your clicker and treats around, you will now have the power to use your clicker whenever your dog does something you like. You can begin to shape his behavior simply by clicking whenever he makes the right choice with his behavior.

For example; you are out in your backyard hanging a load of washing out on the clothesline. You are keeping an eye on your puppy because you don't want him to go into the garden beds, but being the little adventurer that he is, he sneaks up into one. You call him down and once his paws touch the outside ground of the garden bed, you click and reward him with a treat.

Clicker training can be used in both positive ways and to help him understand the negative things that he is doing, or the behaviors you want him to stop. One of the most popular ways to stop a dog from constantly barking all the time, is with clicker training! The key to stopping negative behaviors with clicker training is to manage situations so that your dog doesn't do the behavior that you desire him to stop.

For example, if your dog jumps all over people when they enter the house begin using your clicker to stop the negative behavior. When someone enters the house, have your clicker ready and a treat and make sure your dog knows you have them! When they enter the house he will be excited but tell him to 'Sit!' as soon as they enter. As soon as his bottom touches the ground, Click! And reward him!

How to capture the behavior

The first step is deciding which behavior it is that you are wanting to reinforce and encourage. Perhaps you want him to sit, or lie down, or go onto his mat, or sit quietly while you eat dinner at the table... The options are endless but the clicker method is all the same.

I suggest starting with a simple behavior such as 'Sit' or 'Lie Down'. Once your puppy learns what the clicker is for, and what it means (Treat!), then you can begin working on more difficult tasks. Once he gets the hang of the clicker, it becomes a game for most dogs. You might find that he begins guessing what you want him to do and trying out new things, all just to hear that click and get that treat!

Once you have your puppy used to the clicker and what it means, start adding in your command. Only add the command once he has realized the behavior you want him to do (in this case, sit). Give the command and wait for him to obey your order. As soon as he obeys you, by putting his rear end of the ground, click and reward him.

One problem lots of clicker trainers have is that they forget to add praise to their training too. Just because you click and reward with a treat does not mean that you can't tell him that he is a good boy, or give him a big pat after a succession of commands obeyed. This is especially important if your dog isn't as food orientated as others, however if this is the case, clicker training may not be the best method for training your dog.

- PUPPY PROBLEMS AND DESTRUCTIVE BEHAVIOR -

As cute as they are, puppies can be extremely naughty. No matter how well trained they are, it is within their nature to chew, dig and play. Their days are spent exploring the world around them, and just like human babies, they do most of it with their mouths. It is instinct and something that comes naturally to them and it is important for them to explore and learn for themselves.

You can help your puppy through this stage and you can also keep your sanity while doing so. You can prevent accidents from happening by changing some of your own habits and also creating good habits for your puppy. This chapter is about changing your habits to help him and also help you understand exactly what is going on with him at any given moment of his development.

Teething & Chewing

Puppies will be born to naturally chew on anything that they can sink their young teeth into. It is normal behavior and one that has gone through generations and generations of dogs, and it won't stop anytime soon.

Chewing on items helps the development of your puppies jaw and helps strengthen his bite. When they are teething (more on this in a second) it can also relieve anxiety and sometimes relieve the pain and discomfort that they are experiencing. If you find your puppy chewing non-stop, it may also be a sign of boredom and you should try playing with him or spending some time training him and wearing him out a little. If he is bored, he may also chew on items that are associated with you, think shoes, clothes, and furniture. This is a clear sign of an attempt to get your attention and it would serve you well to listen and give him the desired attention or this behavior will continue.

Most puppies are born without teeth and will begin to develop them in the first month of their life. They will continue to grow new teeth right up until they are about 6 months old.

Below is a rough timeline of a puppy teething schedule:

- 0 - 2 weeks - No teeth yet.
- 2 - 4 weeks - Small teeth (incisors) at the front of the mouth will develop. Some pups will also develop premolars and molars between 3 - 6 weeks. Canines may also develop early with one on each side on both the top and bottom of the mouth.
- 5 - 8 weeks - The final molars appear and the puppies adult teeth will begin pushing out their 'milk teeth'.
- 8 - 16 weeks - Your puppy will be home by now and you will find teeth falling out around your home. Keep a close eye on your puppies teeth as all 28 adult teeth will be coming through and pushing out the puppy tooth.
- 6 months+ - Check your puppies mouth around this age to see if any puppy teeth remain. If so, they will need to be extracted by a veterinarian.

As you can see, the process does go on for a long period of your puppies early life. It is a good idea to provide plenty of chew toys to help ease the pain your pup may be experiencing. This will minimize any potential damage he may cause to your household items.

Now that we have discussed teething, it is important to point out that this may not be the only reason that your puppy is chewing. Most dogs never outgrow chewing, as I mentioned, it is a natural instinct for them to chew.

To prevent inappropriate chewing provide plenty of chew toys for him and keep him well entertained and exercised. If you don't want him to chew your clothing, don't give him old socks or shirts to chew on. Try old milk or egg cartons for cheap toys, as well as stuffed animals with a squeaker inside. Some owners also provide edible chew toys such as rawhide, pigs ears, and bones.

Try rotating your puppies toys every now and then, this will provide new stimulation for him and he won't grow bored of the same toys being available all the time. If he finds an object that you don't want him to chew on, offer a trade and give him something you don't mind him chewing on.

Also, if you see him chewing on something that you don't want him chewing, instead of yelling and telling him off, redirect him to something that he can chew on. Offer a chew toy to distract him and he will slowly learn that if he wishes to chew, he chews the toys you provide, not the furniture.

Digging

We've just gone over chewing and why puppies chew everything they can dig their little puppy teeth into... Now, we're going to cover digging but unfortunately, the concept is exactly the same! Digging comes naturally to dogs, and although you see it as a problem, to him he is just doing what comes naturally to him.

Like with most problem behaviors, there are certain breeds that are more prone to dig than others. In might be built into the DNA of your puppies breed and that will make your job of curbing his behavior more difficult.

The first step of trying to solve any problem behavior that your puppy is displaying is to work out why they are behaving that way. Are they bored? Do they need more exercise? Is he just searching for attention? Are they trying to get to something on the other side of the fence? It might be hot outside and you haven't provided enough shade for him to sleep in, in turn he will dig the top layer of soil to provide a cooler layer for him to lay in.

There are many reasons he may be digging, however in my experience, most puppies dig because they are bored. Puppies also tend to view the yard as their territory and not yours. This is due to them doing most of their 'business' there, and you don't do yours out there. Many dogs also eat outside, therefore it soon becomes their 'den'. This is why they won't mind digging around in the backyard, after all, it is theirs (according to them)!

So how can you stop this behavior before it goes too far and you come home to all your beloved flowers torn to shreds and covered in a pile of dirt? It will take time like everything that tests your puppies natural instincts. But you can do it, just like you can do everything else in this book.

The first step I recommend would be to simply watch him as he wonders around the yard. What does he do? Where does he go and where does he stop to sniff? Keep note of these areas as you will probably find these will be your 'problem spots' that he will dig in. You should also observe his behavior when he settles on his favorite spots, does he sniff for awhile then scratch at the surface? While observing it is ok to tell him off if he starts to dig too much, a loud noise and a good distraction (like a stick or chew toy) will do perfectly for now and it will go a long way to teaching him that digging is not ok.

After observing him for a day or so it is time to start correcting his soon-to-be bad behavior. One of the things you might have noticed when observing him is that the moment he goes to dig, his nose is down on the ground sniffing around. This is key and this will be your main way to stop him digging.

Many owners have found the best way to stop a puppy from digging is to place a substance that is unpleasant to smell for him. Things like paprika, cayenne pepper or apple cider vinegar are perfectly ok and won't hurt him if he decides they don't phase him. Other owners simply place some waste from the dog's usual toilet spot in the hole as dogs will not go near their own waste.

Now, you can't always be outside with your puppy. You might be inside cooking dinner while keeping an eye on him through a window. You see him start to dig so you clap or yell but he doesn't hear you, what can you do??? Buy an air horn. Yes, that's right, get an air horn. You can stay inside and have it by your side ready to catch him in the act, once you see him starting to paw at the ground, grab it and squeeze it. He will hear it, trust me. And he will stop in his tracks to work out what on earth that noise was.

If all this fails you might need to start looking at his exercise schedule. You might not be wearing him out enough. If he has been for a long walk or played fetch in the yard for an hour, he will simply not have enough energy to be digging a big hole in your backyard. This is important and you could simply jump to this step because, in my honest opinion, it is the easiest way to combat a digging puppy. Wear him out and you will find fewer holes in your yard, I promise.

It might also prove worth your time to leave toys laying around your yard for him to find and enjoy. Things like ropes, tree branches and balls are all good and will distract him from the lure of digging. Encourage him to play with these toys when you are out there with him and whenever you catch him digging, have one of the toys nearby ready to distract him with.

One final word on digging, much like the golden rule of housetraining...

Never drag your dog back out to the scene of the crime. Unless you catch him digging, he will not know why you are taking him back out and shoving his nose in a hole. All this will do is teach him to fear you and your yard. This will do more harm than good and please don't do this. By all means, if you catch him in the act, scold him and use the distraction method of changing his behavior but never hit him.

Escaping & Running Away From Home

There is nothing worse than roaming the streets looking for your dog. You're worried sick that something bad has happened and you'd do anything to get him back, safe and sound at home with you. Unfortunately, this is commonplace for some dog owner as dogs do have a tendency to be excellent escape artists. Some owners are also prone to being somewhat ignorant and not being aware of their yard and the potential routes their dog may take to get out.

Like all of the problems we have discussed, you will need to work out why your dog is behaving this way and find a solution to help keep him safe. This is a potentially fatal problem behavior as your dog will have no sense of how to cross a road, which places to stay away from or perhaps he can't swim and he could fall into a flowing river near your house. Life outside the controlled environment of your yard is all potentially dangerous to your dog and if he escapes, you will not be there to keep an eye on him.

You can't always be there at home with your dog. But if you have followed my puppy proofing steps, then your yard should be safe and secure. If he is still getting out you will need to go back through the steps and work out why. Is he jumping the fence? Has he dug his way under the fence? Is there a hole in the fence? Does the latch no longer work on the gate? Whatever it might be, you need to find the problem and provide a solution.

Now, you might fix the problem only for him to go and find a new way to exit your yard. It would be at this point that I begin asking more questions as to why he is trying to get out.

Some common reasons for him to escape might be that he is:

- Bored
- Looking for a mate
- Hunting

- Scared

Most of the time you can narrow these down by knowing your daily routine with your dog. If you take him for a daily walk and depending on the breed, perhaps 2 walks, then you could rule out that he is bored. This would be plenty of exercise and should be enough to keep him occupied and happy inside the perimeter of your yard.

If you have a boy dog, they can go wandering around looking for a female mate. This goes for dogs who have been neutered also, especially if there is a female dog nearby who is on heat. Your dog will be able to pick up their scent and will want to go searching for them. Females on heat might also go looking for a mate, so this problem is not limited to just male dogs. Neutering will reduce this problem, so if you find your unneutered dog escaping and going to the neighbor's house all the time, it might be worth looking into desexing your puppy.

Dogs, especially puppies, love to chase wild animals. Be it a rabbit, a bird, a lizard or a squirrel, they want it and they won't stop until they get it! This is again a natural instinct for many breeds, as there have been generations of their ancestors who have had to hunt for their food. In this case, I would suggest assessing your fence and making sure it is high enough to stop your dog jumping over it. This may be a problem that surfaces after your puppy has grown to their full size and has grown stronger and can jump much higher.

Loud noises can cause different behaviors for your puppy and grown-up dog. Unfamiliar and loud noises such as fireworks can set off your dog and scare them. If they get so scared, they may try to escape your yard in an attempt to run away from the noise. Even the calmest dog can become victim to this, so if you know that there are going to be fireworks (like New Year's Eve) it is a good idea to keep your dog indoors.

If you have tried everything and your dog still seems to be escaping I would recommend strengthening your relationship through training. The more they respect you, the less likely it is that they will go searching for more. Plus, a well-trained dog who escapes, can always be obedient enough to return home by themselves.

Aggressive Behavior

Aggressive behavior in your puppy is a sign for serious concern. If he is regularly growling, snaring or biting you, you will need to get onto the problem quickly and effectively before it becomes a serious issue.

It is important to note the difference between a puppy playfully biting or 'mouthing' at you when you are playing and a serious bite. Puppies will want to bite down and chew, especially when they are teething. However, if this action is paired with growling and aggression you need to implement a change in his behavior.

If you have worked out that your puppy is in fact aggressive by nature, it is time to work out exactly what causes them to be upset. There are many different reasons that puppies get angry, things such as territory, protecting their pack (you), possessions, fear and defense are all common reasons for bad behaviors. Learning to note what is making your dog act this way is the first step in solving this problem. Watch him closely as he plays or wanders around, what sets him off? Is he looking for trouble or trying to avoid it? Does he look scared? Is he scared of people? Or certain types of people (eg children, men, women, etc)?

Once you have learned what the issue is, it is time to fix the problem. You will do so by using all the same training techniques that you have already covered. This includes positivity, not punishment and aggression. Don't try to solve your dog's aggression by being aggressive. Don't ask him to stop growling by growling at him. This sends the wrong message to him and will only cause confusion, making it harder to train him out of the habit.

For example, if your dog is aggressive towards new people that they meet begin your training by standing far enough away from the person so that your dog can see them. You should stand far enough away so that your dog doesn't feel threatened and begin to growl or bark at them. If he does, take some steps backwards. Once he settles and is sitting looking at the stranger but not being aggressive, reward him! Give him a treat, heck, give him two treats and big pats! Once you start to do this your once-upon-a-time aggressive dog will begin to associate strangers with treats and in turn, will think they are fantastic - not threatening!

If you have tried training and you simply don't seem to be getting anywhere, it might be worth taking your dog to the vet to get him assessed for any underlying medical conditions. A medical condition could be making him feel uncomfortable or in pain, which could be causing him distress. Also, consider hiring a professional trainer to assist you with aggressive behavior. They should know excellent techniques and ways to overcome aggressive problems in your dog.

Obviously, this is just one example, and your dog might be aggressive in a completely different way. My advice would be to do some research on the type of aggression you are experiencing, it is my intention to write a book completely dedicated to this topic as I feel very strongly about it. All dogs can be trained out of aggressive behavior and rehoming them isn't always the best option. Please sign up to my mailing list (link in the back of the book) if you would like to be updated with new releases about this topic.

Barking, Whining and Noise

A constantly barking dog is very irritating. I think we have all been there before, sitting inside the comfort of your own home, only to be frustrated by the sound of a constantly barking or whining dog. This barking or whining is a natural behavior for all dogs, it is their way of expressing their emotions, exactly like us when we talk or use our voices to express our feelings.

Dogs should bark, and it would be unwise to teach your dog to never ever bark. Believe it or not, there is such a thing as 'debarking surgery' whereby a veterinary surgeon performs a medical procedure on your dog removing part of your dogs vocal cords. Now, this is my opinion and feel free to disagree with me, but this is completely over the top. All dogs can be trained not to bark, and if you are sending your pooch off for debarking surgery, you are simply being lazy and you are not willing to spend a short amount of time teaching your dog when it is ok to bark and when it is not.

If you notice that your puppy is barking a lot, it is a good idea to get on top of it before it becomes a bad habit for him. Teaching him a 'Quiet!' command is the perfect solution and is something covered in this book. This technique is hard to teach, but with patience and consistency, you can do it.

Some other reasons your dog may be barking include:

- Fear - loud noises, unfamiliar people or fireworks are all things that can cause fear in your dog and cause him to bark out of being scared.
- Loneliness - If your dog has separation issues he will tend to bark a lot. He will bark mostly when you are away so it may be difficult to know that he is doing it. Provide him with plenty of mental and physical stimulation to combat this form of barking.
- Territorialism - Dogs will feel protective over their area, or territory. This could range anywhere from their bed, to the backyard. If a new and unfamiliar person comes near they may bark.

Like any training you do with your dog, you will need to take the right approach to rid him of this undesired behavior. If your dog is barking too much or barking at something that is not normal, the first step is to remove him from those situations which cause him to bark. If he still barks, distract him. Tell him to sit, or stay and throw a ball and play with him instead. Then reward him for that behavior. He will soon learn that barking is not ok and if he doesn't bark he will get more attention than if he does bark.

One of the most important things is to ignore him when he is barking. Wait for him to stop, then give him your attention and use the pause in his bad behavior to curve his behavior. When he stops barking, that is your chance to teach him to fetch instead, or sit or play with you. Distract him and he will soon get the idea.

Never hit him or throw things at him to stop him from barking. This may seem like common sense, but I've seen my share of dog owners do this repeatedly and wonder why their dog still barks at shadows. This approach simply teaches them that they will get attention if they make noise, simple as that. I don't like the idea of shock collars either, I feel like if you follow proper training techniques you don't need to use something that will hurt him and be painful.

- GROOMING YOUR PUPPY -

KEEPING SHINY AND CLEAN!

One of the most enjoyable bonding times that you will get with your new puppy is when you are grooming him. There are plenty of dog owners out there who do not enjoy this part of dog ownership, but I suggest you try to embrace it. It can be very rewarding, for both you and your puppy.

Like humans, dogs need to be groomed to maintain a good level of hygiene. Grooming is not limited to a brush once a week, but also includes bathing, nail trimming, ear cleaning and of course hair cuts! It is a good idea to establish a grooming routine early in your puppies life. This way you get him used to being brushed, being wet, getting his nails trimmed and all that comes with maintaining his hygiene.

Some breeds enjoy grooming while others tend not to be too enthusiastic about it. This isn't limited to brushing either. Although your dog mightn't mind being brushed, when you go to get the hose out and give him a bath it could be an entirely different story. I will touch on all aspects of grooming your puppy in this chapter to hopefully give you a better understanding of what to do and how best to do it.

Brushing Your Dogs Fur

Now, I'm going to make a statement that some of you will curse and scream at me for making - dogs love to be brushed! This is, of course, a pretty broad statement and does not include all dogs. But, that vast majority of dogs, if exposed to being brushed at an early age learn to love a good grooming session.

If you use the proper techniques and use the right equipment, there is no reason that your dog shouldn't enjoy being groomed by you. It is a great bonding session for both of you. You make him feel good about himself while effectively giving him a massage, and you feel good about him sitting there being a good boy.

Your puppies grooming requirements will change as he gets older and the amount of time you need to spend brushing will depend greatly on what type of fur he has and how long it is.

See below for a rough guideline of how often to brush your dog based on his fur type.

- Long Haired - Daily brushing to prevent matting and tangling. During shedding season, it doesn't hurt to do it twice a day.
- Medium Haired - If prone to matting and shedding, twice weekly. If your dog's fur doesn't clump or tangle, once a week should suffice.
- Short Haired - Every few weeks.

Using the guide above, you should begin to work out a routine for you and your puppy. It is of course, only a guide and if you find that your puppy enjoys being brushed then, by all means, make it part of your daily routine. It may soothe your puppy and help calm them down after a big play or you can use it simply for bonding time. Don't limit yourself to the guide I have provided, that is simply a basis on which you should do as a minimum.

To help you work out how often you should brush, I will briefly go through the different types of fur which can be broken down into 5 groups. If you already know which category your puppy will fall into then skip ahead.

- Smooth Coat - Requires the least amount of attention but still needs brushing every so often. This type of hair is close to the body of the dog, for example, a Dachshund, Jack Russell or Beagle. They may shed a lot of fur at times, so try using a de-shedding shampoo and conditioner. Brush him with a bristle brush going against the lay of the hair, then repeat going with the lay of the hair.
- Double Coat - This coat has a soft underlayer and a more coarse outer coat. Normally the outer layer will repel water and dirt however it is a fairly high maintenance coat to take care of. Double coats can be short or long. For short-haired double coats, use a pin brush against the lay of his fur first, the go with the lay on the repeat. For longer and thicker double coats you will need to break it down into sections and try using an undercoat rake to get all the tangles undone. Try using a detangler on the undercoat to loosen any tangles that have formed and finish off by brushing the top coat with a wide-toothed comb. Breeds with this styled coat are: Australian Shepherd, Siberian Husky and Shiba Inu.
- Long Coat - Long coated dogs, such as a German Shepherds or Afghan Hounds, need brushing daily pretty much year-round. These coats can feel coarse or silky but both require a good bath before detangling as this will help ease any pain your dog might feel when brushing. Try using a combo of a pin brush first then a smooth bristle brush second to get the best brush for your long coated dog.
- Wire Coat - Wiry coats are subject to tangling and require a brush a few times a week if possible. These coats will need a stripping comb and a smooth bristle brush to be most effective. You can use a detangler to get out any mats as required. These dogs are hard to groom, so consider doing what you can at home and take them to a professional dog groomer every month or so to get the job done properly. Dog breeds with this type of coat include: Irish Terrier, Scottish Terrier and Otterhounds.
- Curly Coat - These coats are normally very thick and soft. The curls rest close to the body and can be difficult to groom. I highly recommend visiting a professional if you do not feel comfortable maintaining this type of coat, but if you wish to attempt it make sure you have a good, soft brush that can get right down into the curls.

Poodles and Irish Water Spaniels have this type of coat.

Bathing Your Dog

Bathing your dog is another essential part of maintaining healthy hygiene levels. Bathing will keep your dog's coat clean and healthy as well as removing dirt, parasites, and other things that get stuck to your dog's coat. Unlike humans, dogs don't need a bath every day to stay hygienic, but the breed of your particular puppy will determine how often they need to be bathed. Things such as the thickness and length of their fur, how much time they spend outdoors and what they do when they are outside will determine how often you should give them a bath.

Exposing your dog to bathing at a young age will assist you later in life, as some dogs don't like being wet. Alternatively, some breeds get very excited when water is around, so you will need to train them to sit still during bath time.

Make sure you have the right equipment to make bath time a bit easier for both you and your dog. Try to get it all in one easy-to-reach spot when you begin, so you don't have to keep leaving to grab things that you have forgotten.

What you need:

- Tub or sink big enough for your dog to stand up in comfortably
- Shampoo and conditioner (get the dog-friendly type - don't use human shampoo or conditioner)
- Brushes and Combs
- Towels - get enough for drying plus one for your dog to stand on when you get him out. Always get more than you think you will need, this will save extra trips back inside.
- Eye lubricant (known as artificial tear ointment) - this will protect his eyes from shampoo.
- Old clothes. You will get wet, so wear clothes that you won't care about if they get ruined.

Step-by-step Bathing Process

It is a good idea to establish a routine for you and your dog right from the first bath you give him. This will help him learn exactly which stage you are at, and how much longer he will need to be still for. Your dog's bath shouldn't be longer than 10-15 minutes (at most), any more than this they will certainly start to get restless and they might start to play up.

The first step is to brush your dog before you start. Try to remove any tangles and mats that have formed since his last brush as these will be more difficult to get out once he is wet. Once you have given him a brush, apply the eye ointment to protect his eyes from the shampoo.

Now it is time to move on to getting his entire body wet. Try to make sure the water is warm as your dog won't appreciate being bathed in cold water. If you are bathing outside, try to bathe when the weather is warm and the sun is out. I find using a hand-held sprayer is the best way to get the entire body covered and it is much easier to use than a bucket. If your dog is a breed that has a water-resistant coat (eg Labrador) it might take a bit of extra water to get their coat wet all the way through.

When getting their coats wet, do your best to avoid getting water inside your dog's ears and their eyes. They might try to shake the water off, this is their instinct but you can assist in stopping them from doing this by placing your hand on top of their head gently.
After they are completely wet, apply the dog shampoo. It is a good idea to use a shampoo that is soap-free and a general rule is the fewer ingredients the better. For dogs with skin problems try using a shampoo which contains aloe and oatmeal. When you are applying the shampoo, avoid his face, eyes and the genital areas. You should have enough shampoo for it to foam up and be lathered across his body evenly. Apply small amounts at a time rather than one big amount at the start.

Once all of his body has an even amount of shampoo it is time to rub-a-dub-scrub! Give your dog a massage for at least a couple of minutes. Move all over his body and pay attention to any areas you know are particularly dirty. Most dogs enjoy this part of the bath, I mean, they are getting a nice massage after all!

Try to keep your dog comfortable during this time and try to get him not to shake at all. You want the shampoo to be kept in for around 5-10 minutes.

After you have finished lathering his whole body and you are satisfied he is clean it is time to rinse him. Use the same technique that you did when getting him wet, however, take extra care now not to get the shampoo in his eyes or ears. You need to thoroughly rinse all the shampoo out and this can take around 5 minutes. If your dog has folds or creases in his skin make sure you get all the shampoo out of there as it might dry and irritate his skin if not removed.

To rinse the shampoo out use lukewarm water, like when you were getting him wet. After most of the shampoo is out, turn the temperature down to a slightly cooler temperature. This will assist in closing his pores after the clean and remove any leftover shampoo residue.

Now, let your dog out onto the mat you have laid out for him. Stand back for a few seconds and let him shake a couple of times. After he seems satisfied go in with your towel and try to remove as much water as you can. Most dogs will want to run off and rub up against anything they find at this stage and you might find he wants to rub against your legs too.

You can attempt to blow dry your dog if he allows it. Be sure to turn the heat down on the blow-dryer, and don't blow in his face or ears.

After he is completely dry give him another brush and remove any oils or greasy film that might be leftover from the shampoo. Give your dogs eyes a wipe with a slightly damp cloth and try to keep him out of the dirt until he is completely dry.

Trouble Bathing Your Dog?

Some dogs do not like to be bathed. No matter how early you start, or how many treats you give him, some dogs will simply never get used to it.

If this is the case for you and you find you are wrestling him more than you are bathing him, then either ask a friend for help or consider taking him to a professional grooming parlor.

Nail Trimming

Now let's be honest, most dog owners freak out at the idea of trimming their dog's nails. However, it is just as important as brushing and bathing for your loveable pooch and you need to do it. If you don't feel comfortable doing it, you will need to visit the vet to get it done or find a professional groomer who is willing to do it for you.

Dogs nails grow just like human nails. They will wear down more than ours though, as they walk on the pavement, gravel, and concrete. Unless your dog spends most of his time outside though, this won't be enough to allow him not to require a nail trim every now and then.

If you leave your dogs nails to grow, they will curl and start to grow under their paw pads. Obviously, this is very painful for them and can lead to bad infections and it will require medical treatment which will be both horrible for your dog and financially bad for you.

There are a variety of different nail trimmers out on the market, and the type you require will depend on the breed of your dog and their nails. I would encourage you to speak to your vet to see which style they would recommend, mainly because even two dogs of the same breed might have different requirements due to the shape of their paws or the way that their nails grow.

The 3 most common styles of trimmers are:

- Guillotine Style - very beginner friendly and the most commonly used.
- Scissor Style - work just like a regular pair of scissors, normally used on smaller nails.
- Plier Style - Resembling garden pruners, easy to use and last a long time. Available in small, medium and large.

It will serve you well to search and look at the makeup of a dogs nail, especially if your dog has dark colored nails as you may not be able to see the inside contents of the nail. A dogs nail is made of a few different layers. There is a hard outer shell and then a soft cuticle. In the center of the cuticle, there is a nerve and blood vessel. This cuticle is often referred to as the 'quick' and when cut, this can cause the nail to bleed and may be painful for your dog. The best way to avoid this is to cut 2 - 3mm away from the quick, or where you can't see the quick (in darker colored nails), cut where the nail begins to curl.

To begin cutting your dogs nails, get in a good position and have all the equipment ready. Grasp your dog's paw firmly but don't squeeze too hard as this will be uncomfortable for him. It is a good idea to use your dominant hand to hold the trimmers and hold his paw with your other hand. Place your thumb on the bottom of his paw pad and your fingers on the top side of his paw, right up close to his nails. Line up the trimmers to the correct spot as outlined above, and squeeze your trimmers in one smooth motion. Make sure your dog is still when you cut and don't hesitate as this may cause problems.

If your dog starts bleeding it means you may have nicked the quick. The blood vessel has been damaged, however, this isn't a serious injury and you can quickly fix it with some cornstarch or styptic powder. Use a cloth or tissue to wipe away as much of the blood as possible and pack some of the powder onto the nail tip.

If you have clipped the quick, it will be painful for only a short period of time for your dog. They should not have any trouble walking afterwards and if they show any signs of discomfort from the accident you should visit your veterinarian immediately.

Ear Cleaning

Ear cleaning is another part of maintaining healthy hygiene for your dog. All dogs need to have clean ears, and some require cleaning more often than others. It is an easy task to perform yourself at home, and most dogs don't mind having their ears cleaned providing you are gentle and offer an ear massage while you're at it!

You do need to take care when cleaning their ears and if enough care isn't taken, you can damage your dog's ears and cause serious damage. It is easy to clean your dog's ears while you bath them, and it can help them relax if they are difficult to bath as it takes their attention away from being wet.

Before you start cleaning your dog's ears you should visually inspect them and see how dirty they are. You will also need to make sure there is a clear path for you to clean effectively, and if there is hair in the way you might need to remove it by plucking it with your fingers or tweezers. Plucking the hairs on the inside of their ears can be both painful and annoying for your dog if you don't do it right, so try to watch some videos or ask a local groomer for tips.

After the ears are free of any obstacles it is time to get out your ear cleaning solution. This is available at most veterinary surgeries or at your local pet supply shop. Next, pull up your puppies ear flap and squirt a few drops of the ear cleaner on the inside of the ear flap, right next to the ear opening.

Now, gently place the cleaning solution into his ear and squeeze gently. Once you've applied the appropriate amount, begin massaging the base of his ear. This is the part of his ear where the ear cartilage meets his jaw. Once you start massaging you should begin to hear a 'smacking' sound.

Your dog will probably want to shake his head at this stage but try to get him to settle for a few seconds while the solution fills the ridges and canals. By doing this, you allow the solution to loosen any ear debris and wax that has built up. After a few seconds, you can let your dog shake his head but be aware of the liquid coming from his ear, it will be dirty and pretty gross so have a towel close by.

Once he has had a good shake, wipe the ear with a cotton tip. You can also use your finger to remove any debris that has been left on the ear flap. While cleaning up, never place anything down any farther than you can see. After the ear is visually clean, move onto the other ear and repeat the process.

Don't forget to reward him and have treats handy so you can comfort and reward him for behaving himself. He will learn to love the cleaning process if you make it fun and rewarding for him.

- FINDING THE RIGHT VETERNARIAN -

FIND A VET YOU TRUST

Your puppy will have many visits to the vet in the first year of their life. Hopefully, they are all positive visits, and just check-ups and vaccination appointments, but puppies being puppies, you may have to go for other reasons too. Your veterinarian is another family doctor, so you should choose one that both you and your puppy seem to like.

Puppies get up to all sorts of mischief, as we have discussed already in this book. This includes chewing on things, digging and jumping over fences or obstacles that they shouldn't jump over. All of these activities put your puppy at risk of hurting themselves, so having a good Vet on your side might be very beneficial down the track.

There are lots of different Vet's out there, some specializing in a particular animal, or even particular breeds of animals. There are also many different types of Veterinary Surgeries which all vary in size and vary in what types of procedures and appointments that you can attend. You will need to make a conscious decision on what matters most to you in terms of the level of care that is provided for your puppy and the cost that you are willing to pay for that care.

There may be a brand new, whizz-bang, top-notch facility in your town, but they charge double the price of the surgery across the street from them. The surgery across the street might have a Veterinarian working there who has worked in the industry for 20+ years, while the new surgery might be a student straight out of college with next to no on-the-job experience.

These are all decisions that only you can make, much like deciding which school to send your children to.

I would recommend talking to family and friends about their experiences with vets in your area. They might be able to offer a great insight into exactly what you are looking for and they might have heard stories or dealt with particular places that you might not have considered. Your friends and family will be able to share their own experiences and how their dogs took to particular individuals and how that individual handled their dog. This is very important because you need to know that your dog will like your vet.

Another modern day step would be to do a search on the internet. Set aside a few hours a week or two before your puppy comes home and start searching online for vets nearby. Read reviews and look at maps to see exactly where they are located. Be sure to try and read the reviews where possible, and take star ratings with a pinch of salt. Read the details listed in the reviews and this will help define exactly the kind of customer that was either satisfied or dissatisfied. Did they have a similar dog to yours? Or a completely different animal? This all matters and it is worth paying attention to.

While you are online, be sure to check out the websites of all the surgeries that you are considering attending. These normally provide a very good insight as they list all the staff that work there and sometimes list their qualifications and where they received their qualification. It might also list how long they have worked in the industry and where they have worked previously. You might also be able to get a sneak preview of the facilities available at that particular surgery.

After you have narrowed down your options, it doesn't hurt to call the offices and talk to them directly. Tell them your situation, you are about to adopt a puppy, or you already have him at home etc. Ask any questions that you have and try to get a feel for how you might be treated should you become a client there. Are they being helpful? Are they answering your questions? Are they friendly?

The final step in the process would be to make a quick visit to the final candidates. You may have narrowed your choices down to one or two by now, so this shouldn't take you too much time. You may need to make an appointment for this, especially if you are going to ask for a tour or any specialized attention. If you already have your puppy, you may just want to make an appointment, even if the appointment is just to introduce your puppy to the vet. Most vets love this, they get to pat a cute puppy and get paid for it, so you shouldn't have any problems organizing this!

You should try and make the appointment with the vet that you would like to deal with on a permanent basis. There will be no use showing up and getting to know someone who will not be dealing with your dog. Once you have your appointment some things to look out for or ask the vet might be:

- Their education and experience - you might already know this from previous research but doesn't hurt to ask them again.
- How long they've been at that particular clinic
- Their manner and level of professionalism - they should be friendly and interactive with both you and your dog.
- Communication skills - they need to be able to explain what they are doing and why they are doing it. You also need to be able to understand what they are saying. Make sure they also listen to what you are saying or requesting and not dismissive of your concerns.

It may take some time, but choosing the right vet for you is an important part of dog ownership and something that you shouldn't overlook. Go through these processes and you should find a suitable candidate for your puppy. At any stage, if you find yourself feeling underwhelmed by your vet, it is never too late to change. Be aware of your dog's feelings when doing this, and don't chop and change all the time as this will get confusing for them.

- FINAL WORDS -

GOOD LUCK ON YOUR PUPPY TRAINING JOURNEY!

There is so much more that I could cover in this book. I could write for days and days about dogs and how much I adore them. How you get happiness from your relationship with your dog is in your hands.

Treat your dog with love, love them and they will love you back twice as much. A dog truly is Mans Best Friend, so enjoy the journey you go on, try to make light of the bad times (no one enjoys cleaning dog poo!) and make the most of the good times.

Follow this guide to the best of your ability. I strongly urge you to seek help if you find yourself getting frustrated, please don't give up on your puppy. He will learn at his own pace, and as we've discussed, this pace varies from breed to breed and from each individual dog.

I have enjoyed putting this guide together and I hope that it helps you with your puppy training journey. I have plans for many more guides, so please feel free to sign up to my newsletter list to be notified whenever I release a new book.

For now, keep this book close by. Keep referring back to it as you need, and keep at it. You can train your puppy to grow up to be a good dog.

I wish you luck on your puppy training journey - and we'll see each other again in many new books.

Thank you.